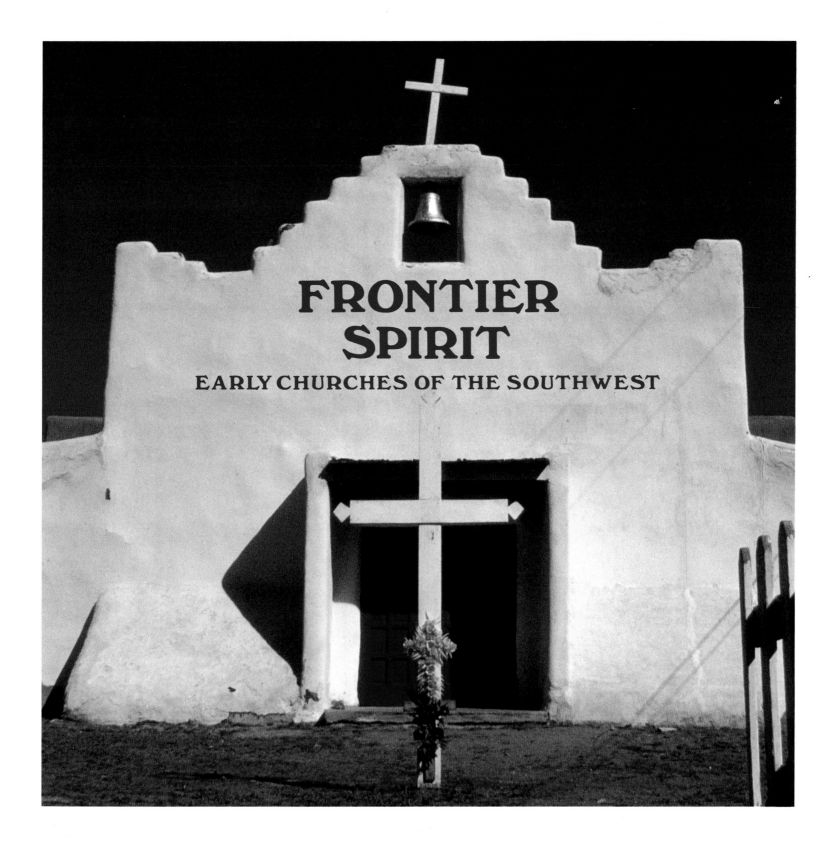

FRONTIER SPIRIT

EARLY CHURCHES OF THE SOUTHWEST

FRONTIER SPIRIT
EARLY CHURCHES OF THE SOUTHWEST

Photographs
and Text by

DOUGLAS
KENT
HALL

Abbeville
Press
Publishers
New York

To Alfred Bush

Editor: **Alan Axelrod**
Designer: **Nai Y. Chang**
Production supervisor: **Hope Koturo**
Maps by: **Sophie Kittredge**

Copyright © 1990
Cross River Press, Ltd.

Printed and bound in Japan
Published in the United States of America by
Abbeville Press, Inc.
First edition

JACKET FRONT, HALF-TITLE PAGE, FRONTISPIECE, TITLE PAGE:
San Lorenzo de Picurís, Picurís pueblo, New Mexico.
The church collapsed in 1986 and is currently being rebuilt.

JACKET BACK:
San Xavier del Bac, Tucson, Arizona

CONTENTS:
Detail of a bulto depicting San Antonio,
from El Santuario de Chimayó—
Nuestro Señor de Esquípulas

Library of Congress Cataloging-in-Publication Data
Hall, Douglas Kent.
    Frontier spirit: early churches of the Southwest/ photographs and text by Douglas Kent Hall.
        p.   cm.
    Includes bibliographical references.
    ISBN 0-89659-914-0 : $55.00
    1. Churches—Southwest, New—Guide-books.
2. Spanish mission buildings—Southwest, New— Guide-books.   3. Southwest, New—Description and travel—1981—Guide-books.   4. Southwest, New—History—To 1848.   I. Title.
F797.H35   1990
979′.01—dc20   89-28342
                                                         CIP

CONTENTS

. . . they built as men must build,

With a sword in one hand and a trowel in the other.

—T. S. ELIOT

INTRODUCTION

San Antonio de Padua, Alcalde, New Mexico

In a field east of the Alcalde morada stand three crosses of los hermanos de luz, the brothers of light, also known as penitentes.

Two miles south of the village where I live lies the site of the first church in North America. The New Mexico Highway Department's sign pinpoints the year of its dedication as 1598 and identifies the place as San Juan Pueblo, a Tewa village on the east bank of the Rio Grande some 30 miles north of Santa Fe.

Nothing remains of the original church structure. There is no description of how it might have looked, nor any indication of whether the Spanish built it specifically as a church or merely appropriated an existing Indian structure for that purpose. Still, this church was the beginning. The churches that grew from it and proliferated throughout the Southwest were destined to leave a mark on the land; not only would they be forerunners of a unique architectural style, they would profoundly affect the people who worshiped in them as well as those who came to admire their beauty.

The churches would flourish, fall into disfavor, be mercilessly remodeled, sometimes beyond recognition, and eventually be restored to their original state. Many of the first buildings would be lost to fire or neglect; they would be demolished to make way for larger churches or simply left to melt, the adobe trickling back into the earth from which it had been formed. However, those churches that remained would find their rightful place in history.

San Juan Nepomuceno, Alcalde, New Mexico

Wasting adobe church at Ojo Caliente, New Mexico

Prior to the expedition that established the territorial capital of Nuevo Mexíco at San Juan, and with it the first church, the Spaniards had been reaching northward for more than half a century, seeking to duplicate the economic successes they had enjoyed in Mexico and South America. Aside from the meanderings of the shipwrecked and stranded Cabeza de Vaca, a strong-hearted, persistent man separated from his band of conquistadors and seeking for some eight years to rejoin them, there had been the well-planned expeditions of Nuño Beltrán de Guzmán, Fray Marcos de Niza, Francisco Vásquez de Coronado, and Antonio de Espejo, as well as at least two unauthorized colonization attempts. The first of these illegal private ventures was led by Gaspar Castaño de Sosa, formerly an alcalde, or mayor, of Monterrey; he was summarily hunted down, brought back to Mexico, put on trial, and sent to the Philippines, where he died in chains. His seat of government at Santo Domingo Pueblo lasted for about a month before it was dismantled by Captain Juan Morlete and his cavalrymen. Failing to learn from Castaño's example, two other privateers, Francisco Leyva de Bonilla and Antonio Gutiérrez de Humana, thrust into New Mexico with their band of followers. They fared no better than Castaño, dying more or less as a result of their own greed. Leyva was killed after a quarrel with his partner, and Antonio Gutiérrez de Humana was killed by the Indians. Still, their efforts signaled the Spaniards' impatience to push north.

Taos Pueblo ruins

The New Mexico territory stood out as a prize. Though no one had ever produced any concrete proof of enormous wealth there, rumors had been voiced for years about the Seven Cities of Cibola and other places beyond them where riches by the wagonload were waiting only to be carried off. These were the kind of stories that fueled the Spanish imagination. The conquistadors saw the Southwest as a vast blank book in which a man might emblazon his name as part of New World history. And when King Philip II decided to open the area to colonization, he was flooded with bids from the most powerful and ambitious noblemen and entrepreneurs in Mexico.

Philip weighed the offers against any projected drain on the royal treasury, around which he is said to have kept a miserly fist. He seesawed between the leading candidates for years, and ultimately awarded the contract to Don Juan de Oñate.

Don Juan was the son of Cristóbal de Oñate, who had distinguished himself in the service of Hernando Cortés and had then gone on to hold the office of captain general in the Kingdom of Nueva Galicia; he had helped to discover and exploit the rich Zacatecas silver mines, a feat that had made him wealthy and had also enriched the royal treasury. Not only had Don Juan followed his father's lead, he had further advanced himself financially and politically by marrying Doña Isabel de Tolosa, whose mother was the daughter of Cortés and whose grandfather was Moctezuma himself, the celebrated ruler of the Aztecs. Don Juan was, by inheritance and by his own labor and ingenuity, a man of wealth, power, and enviable social standing, all of which were undoubtedly instrumental in his gaining the coveted appointment.

From the very beginning, however, the new governorship was plagued with problems, not the least of which were costly delays. Oñate first received approval for his colonization program in 1595, but it was not until 1598, almost three years later, that he was free to act. First, there was the newly appointed viceroy, who questioned the wisdom of granting Oñate all the powers set forth in his original contract. Then the Council of the Indies declared him unfit to assume leadership of the expedition. But, in the end, Oñate was permitted to begin preparations for the long trek north.

Once the new governor-designate had brought the politics of the situation under control and silenced his opponents, his real work began. Travel in the high desert was never easy, and the business of venturing forth to colonize this vast area in the name of God and the Spanish crown was a huge, complex undertaking. It represented a sizable outlay of capital on the part of Oñate and the group of investors who backed him. Each facet of the expedition demanded extensive planning. Every known situation and circumstance had to be explored, every eventuality had to be considered, and precautions had to be taken even in anticipation of the unknown. Vast quantities of food and water were needed to keep the hundreds of men, women, and children and the thousands of livestock moving. Plans had to be made for sickness and accidents.

From a spot near Santa Barbara, Nueva Viscaya—where representatives of King Philip had subjected the caravan to a bothersome inspection in minute detail to assure that Oñate had satisfied his contract down to the last item—the expedition finally creaked into motion.

One can imagine Oñate and his group of elegant riders taking the lead, mounted on the finest horses bred from Spanish stock. Stretching for miles behind them was the caravan, worming its way along, etching an indelible trail into the face of the earth. There were eighty-four carretas, or wagons, loaded with tools, seed, household goods, and other supplies. One hundred and

San José, the Laguna pueblo church, which dates back to the early years of the eighteenth century

Nuestra Señora de San Juan de los Lagos, located in Talpa, New Mexico, off State Highway 3, a few miles northeast of Ranchos de Taos, was constructed in 1827 but has been newly plastered in recent years.

thirty families had been recruited; in addition, there were 270 unmarried men, among them soldiers, tradesmen, farmers, adventurers, and opportunists. At the expense of the king, ten Franciscans had joined the expedition as God's representatives in New Mexico; they would build their churches and bring Christianity to the Indians. There were servants and slaves, camp tenders and wranglers. Then came the animals, some seven thousand of them, in huge herds—cattle, sheep, horses, and goats. It was like a small city in motion, hooves and feet and wheels drumming up dust and filling the sky with a billowing cloud that floated above the whole assembly as it crawled slowly up through what would one day become the Mexican state of Chihuahua.

The contrasts in style and station of the colonists were enormous. They spanned the spectrum of humanity, from the very rich to the poor, from nobleman to slave. It was reported, for example, that one member of Oñate's party had brought in the way of wardrobe and personal belongings the following items:

- Six suits—one cut from blue Italian velvet trimmed with wide gold passementerie, with green silk stockings, blue garters, and points of gold lace; one of purple Castilian cloth; one of rose satin, and another of straw-colored satin; one of chestnut-colored cloth; and the last one of flowered Chinese silk.
- Of his three doublets, two were of dressed kid and one of royal lion skin, which was trimmed in gold. Add to that fourteen pairs of Rouen linen breeches, two linen shirts, and six linen handkerchiefs.
- The most colorful of his three hats was made of purple taffeta trimmed with blue, purple, and yellow feathers and banded with gold and silver passementerie braid.
- For footwear he had forty pairs of boots, shoes, and gaiters.
- He had three suits of armor.
- He had brought thirty horses and mules, four saddles, and three suits of horse armor.
- His weapons included a silver-handled lance with gold and purple tassels, a sword and gilded dagger, a broadsword, two shields, and a silken banner.
- He had packed a bedstead, two mattresses, and ample bedding. To care for his needs and those of his animals, he had brought along a number of personal servants.

Only Oñate himself and a few of his relatives and well-heeled investors would have outfitted themselves to travel in such opulence. However, it is safe to say that most of the people making the journey would have had far less in their possession; many of them, particularly the poor servants and Indians, owned little more than the clothing they wore. The Franciscans, recalling the example of their founder, St. Francis of Assisi, and the vow of poverty they had taken upon entering the Order, traveled with few personal belongings aside from those items they would need to supplement the allotment of materials they had been given for their churches.

Oñate paused at El Paso del Norte and, with great ceremony, took possession of New Mexico. His florid speech was recorded by the King's clerk, Juan Pérez de Donis:

> In the name of the Most Holy Trinity, and the undivided Eternal Unity, Deity and Majesty, Father, Son and Holy Ghost, three persons in one sole essence, and one and only true God, that by his eternal will, Almighty Power and Infinite Wisdom, directs, governs and disposes potently sweet from sea to sea, from end to end, as beginning and end of all things, and in whose hands the Eternal Pontificate and Priesthood, the Empires and Kingdoms, Principalities, Dynasties, Republics, elders and minors, families and person, as in the Eternal Priest, Emperor and King of Emperors and Kings, Lord of Lords, Creator of the heavens and the earth, elements, birds and fishes, animals and plants and all creatures corporal and spiritual, rational and irrational, from the most supreme cherubim to the most despised ant and tiny butterfly; and to his honor and glory and his most sacred and blessed mother, the Holy Virgin Mary, our Lady, I, Don Juan de Oñate, governor and captain general, and adelantado of New Mexico, and of its kingdoms and provinces, as well as of those in their vicinity and contiguous thereto, as settler, discoverer and pacifier of them and of the said kingdoms, by the order of the King, our Lord. I find myself today with my full and entire camp near the river which they call Del Norte, and on the bank which is contiguous to the first towns of New Mexico, and whereas I wish to take possession of the land today, the day of the Ascension of our Lord, dated April 30th, of the present year 1598 . . .

And so on. With this, his first official act in a territory over which he had been given almost absolute power, Don Juan de Oñate

Interior, abandoned church at Ojo Caliente, New Mexico

set the tone of his march up the Rio Grande.

The huge collection of human beings, bizarre wheeled vehicles, and animals proved to be both puzzling and frightening to the Indians. Many fled their villages in terror. Those who stayed behind would certainly have been bewildered by all they saw and heard—the gentlemen in their finery, the soldiers with their armor and strange weapons, the wagons, the herds of domesticated animals. They'd have puzzled, too, at the declaration by Oñate through his translators—whose command of the Indian languages must have been halting and imperfect at best—that he was suddenly taking possession of their land and control of their lives.

From the very beginning, the Spaniards made little or no attempt to understand the Indians or their history. They showed even less curiosity about Indian culture or the very intricate religious fabric that governed every aspect of these people's lives. Conquistadors, soldiers, and priests were all equally bound up in the complex ego of conquerors. They shared the attitudes that had governed earlier crusaders and inquisitors, the attitudes evident in Oñate's speech, and regarded the Indians as savages. They considered the dances and other ceremonies the Indians held sacred as nothing more than crude pagan rites that failed to fit into the pattern of their own narrowly circumscribed Christian worldview. Perhaps if they had taken the time to discover parallels between the Indian beliefs and their own, they might have integrated into Indian religion the elements of Christianity that complemented it and thereby gradually made some important inroads. But the early Spaniards in New Mexico were in a hurry, always fixing their sights on the more immediate goals of wealth, land, slaves, and souls.

There is a long history of Spanish cruelty toward the Indians in the Southwest—even among the priests, of whom it must be said that they most likely believed their suppression of native beliefs was for the good of the Indian people. The Spaniards certainly had no edge over other Europeans so far as cruelty to Indians is concerned. And they offered the church as a kind of balancing agent to offset their rapacity, as they systematically stripped the New World of wealth, transporting it back to Spain by the galleon-load.

The Spaniards saw themselves as enlightened beings, Christians who were superior to the Indians in every way. They were intent on persuading them to give up their ideas, wealth, and freedom. In the Spanish view, the Indians were no more advanced than simple, untutored children. The Spanish purpose was to

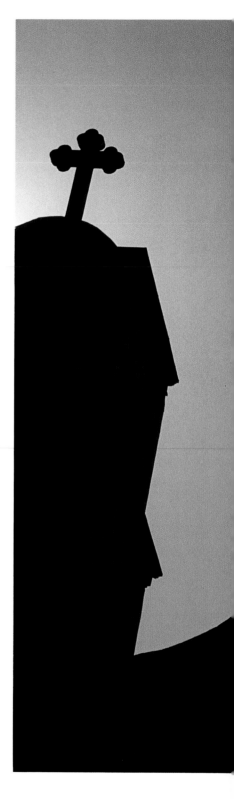

guide them—by force, if necessary—to accept a completely new way of thinking about the world and their place in it. The Indians often saw the advantages of compromise and stoically accepted the teachings offered by the priests, laying the more obvious trappings of Christianity over their own deeper beliefs like a convenient veneer. Not that we know very much about the Indian mind of that time, as most of what we have learned has come to us from the written observations of the Spanish and other Europeans.

Riding ahead of the main caravan as it moved out of El Paso, Oñate and a select group of men made their way almost four hundred miles up the Rio Grande, stopping at pueblo after pueblo. Juan Pérez de Donis, the king's official notary, wrote in a report detailing a meeting between Oñate and a large gathering of Indian leaders at Santo Domingo Pueblo: "He [Oñate] told them that he had been sent by the most powerful king and ruler in the world, Don Philip, king of Spain, who desired especially to serve God our Lord and to bring about the salvation of their souls, but wished also to have them as his subjects and to protect and bring justice to them, as he was doing for other natives of the East and West Indies...."

It was in the same spirit that Oñate rode into the pueblo called Ohke, situated on the east bank of the Rio Grande, between the Jémez and the Sangre de Cristo mountains. He drove the Indians from their dwellings and installed himself and his men in the hastily emptied houses. Renaming the pueblo San Juan de los Caballeros, he made it the first capital of the newly appropriated territory.

San Juan then became the site of the first church in the Southwest and the first church in what would become the United States. It was dedicated eight years before Jamestown was settled and twenty-two years before the landing at Plymouth Rock. Tradition tells us that, during the dedication ceremony, the colonists performed ancient pageants brought from Spain, which possibly included the Cristianos y Moros pageant and the Matachines dance—with additions and embellishments appropriate to the New World, including the characterization of Cortés's powerful Aztec mistress, Malinche, and Oñate's wife's grandfather, Moctezuma, as major figures among the Matachines. The dance had been brought to Spain by the Moors, for whom it was a social ritual; in Spain it gradually took on Christian symbolism and became, over the centuries, an enactment of the contest between good and evil.

San José church and cemetery, Hernandez, New Mexico

Acting in his role as governor with absolute power over all ecclesiastical matters, Oñate divided the territory into seven mission districts and assigned the duty of looking after them to the Franciscans who had traveled in his party. To Fray Alonso de Lugo, he assigned the Jemez and the Apaches, including the Navajos, in the neighboring mountains and settlements. To Fray Francisco de Zamora went the northern pueblos of Picuris and Taos and all of the Apaches who lived from the Sierra Nevada to the north and the east. Fray Francisco San Miguel was given the Pecos pueblo and the other pueblos surrounding it. Fray Juan de Rozas was assigned a number of Keres pueblos, including San Felipe, Santo Domingo, and Cochiti. To Fray Andrés Corchado went Zia, Acoma, Zuñi, and the Hopi villages. Fray Juan Carlos would be responsible for the Tiguex pueblos in the Bernalillo area. A priest, Fray Cristóbal de Salazar, and a lay brother, Fray Juan de San Buenaventura, were assigned San Juan de los Caballeros and the other Tewa pueblos. Fray Alonso Martínez, the father commissary, and Fray Pedro de Vergara, a lay brother, also made their administrative headquarters in San Juan, moving it later to San Gabriel, when that pueblo became Oñate's new base of operations.

These were large missions and represented a huge amount of work, especially as parceled out to so few men. The country was new and relatively unknown. There was the burden of unfamiliar languages. The idea of worshiping gods was basic to Indian life; however, the concept of one God, with all others excluded, was almost incomprehensible. But the Franciscans were diligent and full of high purpose. They wanted to prove themselves equal to the challenges of this country populated by Indians far less cooperative than those they had found in Mexico. In that spirit, their work went forward, and by 1630 they had established twenty-five missions and built as many churches.

The campo santo, or cemetery, at Penasco, New Mexico

FREEHAND ARCHITECTURE

Abandoned adobe church near Black Mesa and San Ildefonso Pueblo, New Mexico

The Franciscans who carried Christianity to New Mexico were pragmatists. Able to thrive on hardship and poverty, they were particularly well suited to the task of creating frontier missions. Each day in the new territory brought fresh challenges, and to meet them the father had to become a jack-of-all-trades. In addition to his familiar calling of priest and teacher, he was expected to undertake the various aspects of building his church; this included assuming the responsibilities of architect-designer and structural engineer, as well as laborer and foreman, working with and overseeing the work done by the Indians.

The weathered adobe of the Black Mesa church

Interiors, Black Mesa

    The Franciscans were resigned and dedicated men. In the most extreme cases, they were prepared to rely upon the charity of their fellow man for everything necessary to their existence. Even so, it must have been a sobering experience for a priest to survey the village in search of a church site, hoping that the space he was measuring would eventually become a holy place, dedicated to worship and learning, rather than an over-sized sarcophagus. The history of previous Franciscan ventures into New Mexico would not have been particularly comforting. The accounts of Franciscans already martyred by the Indians were well known and included the names of Fray Juan Padilla, Fray Luis de Ubeda, and Fray Agustín Ruiz.

    The first problems the priest took on as church architect were capacity and feasibility. He needed to plan a building large enough to house his flock, and he had to consider the kind and quality of building materials that were most readily available in the immediate area. Whatever notions he might have had of aesthetics and decoration could be realized later. On the frontier, the art that graced the early churches was deemed a triumph and a blessing, not a necessity; it had to come in its own time.

Oratorio de San Buenaventura
on the Plaza del Cerro at
Chimayó: interior with altar
screen

No two priests were the same, of course, and whatever church-building skills they possessed depended on their backgrounds. Only a few individuals arrived in New Mexico with experience that might have helped them to become builders. Nowhere in the formal training for the ministry had there been courses in architecture and engineering. Whatever a priest's former experience had been, he suddenly found himself confronted with the monumental task of actually creating a church, of drawing out a rough sketch or—according to his talents—a more detailed plan, and then beginning to build his church from the foundation to the roof.

There was one small concession. As part of an agreement the Franciscan Order had made with the king, at the outset of his mission each priest was issued a standard set of supplies to be used in the building of his church and the convento in which he would live. They were:

10 axes	1 medium-sized saw	6,000 nails
3 adzes	1 chisel	1 dozen hinges
3 spades	2 augers	2 small locks
10 hoes	1 plane	a number of small latches
	1 large latch	

These items, mostly tools and some bare-essential hardware, represented everything the priest was given. Beyond these he was left to his own ingenuity and resourcefulness, and the generosity of his people, to build his church and home.

The only labor, besides his own, came from the people of the village. Indian women, whose traditional work included the construction of their dwellings, were accomplished builders. However, their ideas differed from those of the priests. Their structures were functional, with little or no decoration. They had always created buildings that fit the environment; their houses flowed with the land and maintained an essential harmony with nature. All of their buildings were basically horizontal, mirroring the natural rhythm of mesa and mountain, reflecting a closeness they felt with the place where they lived.

Adobe became the material from which most of the churches in New Mexico were built. Stone was available, especially in the Rio Abajo, where it was used in some early missions, but there were no masons in New Mexico capable of working stone on a large scale, as there had been in Spain and Mexico. Adobe, a building material found in most arid regions of the world, is fairly simple to handle; the builder needs no special tools and little

Lamp on sconce, Chimayó

San Francisco, the cathedral in Santa Fe, the dream of Bishop Lamy, replaced the old adobe church around which the cathedral was contructed and which was dismantled as the stone building took form. Reminiscent of the churches of Europe, but lacking in character, San Francisco seems cold and out of place in the company of the great churches of New Mexico.

training. Fortunately, too, the soil in New Mexico tends to be a mixture of sand and clay that is well balanced for sturdy adobe bricks. In some areas, notably northern New Mexico, straw was added to the adobe mud for better bonding and to facilitate drying. One great advantage of adobe is that the bricks can be formed directly on the ground, near where they are to be used, thereby cutting down on labor and time.

Indian women had worked with adobe for hundreds of years prior to the arrival of the Spanish. Their crude method of building, known as puddling, called for putting up walls by forming layers of mud a few inches thick, sometimes packing stones into the mixture, then allowing the layer to dry before continuing. It was a tedious process and not particularly suited to large struc-

Nuestra Señora de Guadalupe, Velarde, New Mexico

29

tures with high walls. Far more efficient to handle and much stronger is adobe that has been formed into bricks. The priests taught the Indians to make bricks—in itself a significant contribution to the architecture of the Southwest.

The bricks were formed with an adobero, a bottomless wooden box into which the doughlike adobe mud was packed. The adobero was lifted away from the still-damp bricks and filled again and again. After a couple of days, the bricks would have set up enough to be turned on end and thus expose more area to the air and further facilitate the curing. After six or seven days in the hot sun, the bricks could be stacked. Four or five weeks later, the cured adobes, measuring ten by eighteen by five inches and weighing approximately fifty to sixty pounds each, were ready to use. The number of adobe bricks that could be made at one time was limited only by available labor, space, and materials. They could be conveniently stockpiled or they could be dried and then put into walls, which rose far more rapidly than those constructed by the old puddling method. Normally, the bricks were laid up in overlapping courses in the manner of smaller kiln-fired bricks. The mortar was the same mixture of sand and clay used in making the bricks themselves.

One disadvantage of adobe was that, although it dried into surprisingly strong bricks, it was vulnerable to weathering. It had

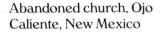

Abandoned church, Ojo Caliente, New Mexico

Fastened to one of the vigas in Our Lady of Guadalupe, Velarde, is this piece from the original church, which was erected in 1617, a fact celebrated in the carved inscription.

to be protected and continually repaired. The original mixture of the adobe had to be balanced with the right amounts of sand and clay. If the clay content was too high, the bricks warped, became brittle, and cracked; if there was too much sand, the bricks were too soft, tending to crumble quickly and weather away.

In many ways, the adobe churches invited, then defied, disaster. Each one was a paradox and a miracle, a stout and enduring fortress constructed from soft and permeable material. The foundation—where a foundation had been laid down—was usually a mere pit filled with courses of adobe bricks or a rubble of fieldstones and adobes.

Women, often helped by their children, became the principal builders of church walls. The men, who felt adobe work was degrading, were willing to help only with bringing the vigas—the trees cut to serve as rafters upon which the roof was laid—and with carpentry jobs that seemed similar to the work they were used to doing, which traditionally included carving ceremonial symbols, masks, and figures, and making boats and traps. Men

felled the trees, brought back the logs, and dressed them for vigas or cut and shaped them into corbels to support the vigas. Logs were also split and worked into lumber for doors, window frames, and shutters; or they were made into furniture needed for the church or the convento.

The typical church was larger than any structure the Indians had built for themselves; it was bigger than their communal ceremonial structures—the kivas—taking up at least as much space as half a dozen of their dwellings. Its walls sometimes rising to a height of thirty feet, the building had incredible volume. The scale of the church seemed to add a sense of grandeur to the village. It was big and solid, rising above all houses

Cristo Rey in Santa Fe, embodying the style of the old adobe churches, was designed by John Gaw Meem and built in this century.

Window at Nuestra Señora de San Juan de los Lagos, Talpa, New Mexico

OPPOSITE AND THIS PAGE:
The main reredos and details
from the altar at El Valle, New
Mexico

and kivas until it became a point of focus, a landmark. Its size added emphasis to its function, visually underlining its importance and making the structure seem to soar.

There were two basic variations on the design of the New Mexican church. The first and most common was a simple oblong box, which could serve both as a house of worship and a fortress; the second was essentially the same box expanded into the shape of a cross, a much grander design that added more capacity and allowed for multiple altars. There were few windows, and those were small. In many cases, a clerestory window was added above the transept to focus light from the roof onto the sanctuary and altar.

Like the church itself, most of the art—aside from those few pieces the priest might have brought from Spain or Mexico—had to be manufactured locally or done without until reredoses (altar screens), retablos (ornamental panels behind the altar), paintings, and bultos (religious sculptures) could be shipped up from Mexico. Often the father made his own altar screens, carved bultos, and created paintings, sometimes with the help of a soldier or one of the colonists. The Indians followed the example of their priest and contributed paintings and carving, frequently adding touches out of their own culture to the Christian imagery that was slowly becoming a part of their lives.

OVERLEAF LEFT:
A bulto of Nuestra Señora de San Juan de los Lagos dominates the reredos at Talpa. It was painted by Molleno. The upper right panel depicts Santiago mounted on a horse; below him is San Antonio de Padua; the crucifix is beneath Nuestra Señora de San Juan de Los Lagos; in the lower left panel is Nuestra Señora de Talpa; and above her is San Bernardo with cross and scepter.

OVERLEAF RIGHT:
Modern shelving holds various santos, many of which are brought to the chapel and left for short periods by various members of the congregation.

PAGE 38:
San Francisco de Asís de las Trampas de Ranchos de Taos

CHURCHES OF NEW MEXICO AND ARIZONA

NEW MEXICO

- CUBA
- TAOS
- RANCHOS DE TAOS
- 21 OJO CALIENTE
- 20
- 22
- 19 ALCALDE
- 18
- VELARDE
- HERNANDEZ
- 17
- PENASCO
- SAN JUAN PUEBLO
- 16 15 14 13
- ESPANOLA
- 7
- 76
- TRAMPAS
- SANTA CLARA PUEBLO
- LOS ALAMOS
- 12
- 11 CHIMAYO
- TRUCHIAS
- 8
- SAN IDELFONSO PUEBLO
- 10 CORDOVA 9
- SANTA CRUZ
- SANGRE DE CRISTO RANGE
- Rio Puerco
- SANTA FE
- 6
- 25
- 5
- Rio Grande
- LAGUNA PUEBLO
- LAS VEGAS
- 4
- 3
- ALAMEDA
- 285
- 84 85
- Rio Colorado
- ALBUQUERQUE
- 40
- ISLETA
- 2
- 84
- BELEN
- N
- CHURCH
- CITY, TOWN
- RIVER
- 15 INTERSTATE HIGHWAY
- 40 U.S. HIGHWAY
- 6 PAVED ROAD
- 60
- 0 MILES 10 20 30 40
- 1
- VAUGHN
- SOCORRO
- 54
- 44
- 4
- 68
- 75
- 3

The great missions, churches, chapels, and oratorios of New Mexico are buildings of uncommon beauty. Not only do they present us with a record of the growth of an architecture at once simple, sculptural, and quite different from the structure of traditional churches, they have also brought forward with them a glimpse of our earliest American history.

Many of the churches of New Mexico were constructed at least a century and a half before the more widely publicized missions of California. They constitute the first and most representative examples of Spanish-conquest architecture in the Southwest, an architecture that expresses in solid form the need, desire, ingenuity, and commitment that fueled the Spanish expansion in the New World.

A number of early travelers to New Mexico found its churches disappointing, however. Some went so far as to label them sorry huts or little mud hovels. They were indeed made of mud—of adobe—and were limited structurally by what this strangely fragile but surprisingly sturdy material could become. Circumstances and change left many of them sadly bereft—such as the wasting Capilla de San Antonio at Alcalde, the ruins of the old church at Ojo Caliente, and the abandoned church near Black Mesa between Santa Clara pueblo and San Ildefonso pueblo. On the other hand, structures such as San Felipe Neri in Albuquerque, Santa Cruz de la Cañada in Santa Cruz, San Francisco de Asís in Ranchos de Taos, and San José de Gracia at Las Trampas are not small, let alone hovels. The early criticism came from people who were comparing an unfamiliar style of architecture to an accepted style with which they obviously felt far more comfortable. Indeed, later travelers have been more generous in their comments. One aptly called the churches examples of "freehand architecture, with the living quality of a sculptor's work."

There is about these buildings an unassuming grace that sets them apart from the more formal churches against which they are usually measured. If they lack the sweep and grandeur of those more sophisticated structures—which were often planned by celebrated architects and built by crews of accomplished craftsmen—they make up for it in the fact that, regardless of size, they are at once one with and part of the land upon which they sit. Each church shows the caring hand of the people who worship in it and whose lives are joined in its history.

SANTA CRUZ DE LA CAÑADA

Bulto of San Francisco in the reredos of La Capilla de San Francisco at Santa Cruz de la Cañada

OPPOSITE:
Santa Cruz de la Cañada, Santa Cruz

The great church of Santa Cruz de la Cañada, dating from 1733, faces due east across the Santa Cruz plaza toward the Sangre de Cristo Mountains. It is laid out in the form of a massive cross. That motif is repeated on the elegant set of huge double doors in front; three white crosses are grouped on each door and surrounded by a total of eight stars. A pitched roof was added at some time in the building's history and is presently covered with corrugated metal, which, in a strange way, mirrors the distant landscape of the Jémez Mountains to the west and lends its own kind of grace to the overall form of the building.

Unlike the early churches in the nearby Indian pueblos, Santa Cruz was not a mission church, though it was sometimes serviced by Franciscan priests from the pueblo missions. Santa Cruz de la Cañada was built by the Spaniards who had come to settle the fertile valley along the Santa Cruz River, and their descendants have kept it alive for nearly two and a half centuries. In 1741, according to the account Fray Francisco Atanasio Domínguez wrote to his superior in 1776, "a widow called Antonia Serna declared and stated that of her own free will she was giving the necessary land for the church, which had already been started, since it was for the religious, and that for their protection and that of the church, she was giving sufficient land in order that in all four directions the citizens might build the houses they liked in the form of streets, with the church in the middle."

In the plaza at Santa Cruz stands a white concrete cross emblazoned with a red heart where the arms intersect. This cross seems to symbolize the strong spirit that has existed here since

Painting of San Francisco in the reredos of La Capilla de San Francisco at Santa Cruz de la Cañada

The main reredos, Santa Cruz de la Cañada

OVERLEAF:
Santa Cruz de La Cañada, from outside the compound walls

the church was built. The plaza is no longer the active place it was when it served as the center of village commerce. Evidence of the life that grew here and thrived for roughly two centuries can, however, be seen in the wasting outlines of old signs. A few faded letters that advertised motor oil, feed, and groceries are still readable on storefronts—small businesses long since supplanted by the shopping centers of Española and the malls of Santa Fe.

Inside Santa Cruz the nave sweeps up to a reredos bathed in soft daylight and dominated by a handsome crucifix carved by José Rafael Aragón (1795–1862), perhaps the most accomplished of the New Mexican santeros (painters and carvers of sacred images). To the far left of this Cristo is a painting of Santa Teresa de Ávila, to the near left is San José con el Niño; on the near right is San Francisco Xavier, and on the far right, Santa Barbara. In the upper left is La Sagrada Familia, and on the right is Santa Rosalía de Palmero. The Capilla de San Francisco is to the south of the main altar. And the larger Capilla de Nuestra Señora del Carmen opens to the north, completing the cross. In a niche on the south side of the nave rests the Santo Entierro, the work of the eighteenth-century resident-priest and artist Fray Andrés Garcés. Facing it from the opposite wall is one of the fine reredoses by José Rafael Aragón. The top panels depict Nuestra Señora de Guadalupe. In the two tiers of panels beneath the virgin are Santa Rita de Cascia, Crucifijo, Santa Rosalía de Palermo, Nuestra Señora de los Dolores, San José con el Niño, and San Lorenzo.

Santa Cruz is rich in examples of the art of José Rafael Aragón, whose work clearly stands out in the New Mexican churches where it appears. Each piece is executed with confidence and a richness of detail, the imagery strong and graced with a sense of piety. The sensitivity in the hands and faces and the feeling in the flow of the garments worn by his figures combine with a skillful use of color—as seen in the painting of San Francisco de Xavier in the main altar screen and the quality of the carving in the bulto of Nuestro Padre Jesús Nazareno that stands on the south side of the nave—to elevate his work to a level far above most of the New Mexican artists of the time. Fortunately, many of his pieces at Santa Cruz that had been overpainted in the century after his death were brought back to their original state in the last decade by judicious restoration.

EL SANTUARIO DE CHIMAYÓ—
NUESTRO SEÑOR DE ESQUÍPULAS

Clockwise, from upper left— Miguel Aragon's painting of San José with the Christ child and a flowering rod; San Juan Nepomuceno; San José with the Christ child; San Antonio with cross and skull; Aragon's painting of Santa Rosalia de Palermo

New Mexico State Highway 76 east out of Española abounds in churches, and the hilltops bristle with the crosses and spires of private chapels. Half a mile west of Santa Cruz is the small Capilla del Santo Niño de Atocha. East of Santa Cruz, in Cuartelez, stands Capilla de la Sangre de Cristo. Just off the highway, on the sadly wasting Plaza del Cerro at Chimayó, is the Oratorio de San Buenaventura, a very fine eighteenth-century chapel, once part of a house, with a packed dirt floor and a small, well-painted altar screen, still in the care of the Ortega family.

El Santuario de Chimayó is located on New Mexico 520, a short distance southeast of the point where it forks away from

El Santuario

Highway 76. The fame of this remarkable church lives on in the hearts of the faithful, who flock to it not only for the annual pilgrimage of Good Friday but with astonishing regularity throughout the year to make its miracle repeat itself over and over.

People come to the Santuario to pray and to lighten the burden of their afflictions. In the sacristy, which is entered through a doorway opening from the left-hand side of the sanctuary, are the sobering vestiges of their visits: crutches, braces, eye patches, plastic hospital ID bracelets, all stacked along walls and in corners, hung on nails, and suspended from the low vigas. On the walls are paintings, drawings, photographs, poems, prayers, news clippings, and announcements left as symbols of hope, the proof of some abiding faith or testament of a personal miracle.

El Santuario is dedicated to Our Lord of Esquípulas, also known as El Cristo Negro, the black Christ. He presides over two shrines famous for their healing—the first in Esquípulas, Guatemala, the second in Chimayó (El Potrero). How this little-known figure came to be the patron of this particular church is the subject of many fascinating stories that have been told through the years in the local community.

In one story, Bernardo Abeyta, who would later take on the responsibility of building El Santuario, is portrayed as a member of Los Hermanos Nazareño—the Penitentes—of Potrero. During Holy Week he was in the hills around Potrero, doing his penance and honoring the holy places, when he saw a bright shaft of light shining from a hole in the ground near the Santa Cruz River. He rushed to where the light shone and there dug out, with his bare hands, the miraculous crucifix of Our Lord of Esquípulas. He called all the local people to see what he had found. Forming a procession, they carried the crucifix to Santa Cruz and presented it to the priest. After hearing the story, he agreed that it should be placed in a niche in the main altar of the mother church at Santa Cruz. The next morning the crucifix was missing from the niche and was subsequently found in the original hole near the river. This same episode repeated itself three times. The people resigned themselves to the fact that the crucifix desired to remain in El Potrero. And, to honor it, a chapel was built above the hole where it had first appeared.

A second story tells of a small and kindly priest who was in the habit of wandering through the foothills carrying a large wooden cross. One day he was stopped by Indians and killed. Some Spanish soldiers found him and buried him with his cross in a grave they made near the river. Years later, following a winter of heavy snows, the river flooded, washing the dirt out of the grave. The people of El Potrero found the cross in the hole and took it to the priest in Santa Cruz. Again there were three trips back and forth between Potrero and Santa Cruz with the cross, which returned mysteriously to the hole each time. And, again, the decision was made to build the chapel upon the spot where the crucifix obviously wanted to remain.

In a third story, Bernardo Abeyta, gravely ill, is said to have been outside one morning in early spring, bundled in blankets

Votive candles to the right of the main reredos

The main reredos at El Santuario, painted by Molleno, "the chili painter," with the Cristo Negro de Esquípulas

Detail from main reredos

Detail of painting from the main reredos at El Santuario depicting the Franciscan emblem of the arm of Jesus Christ crossed with the arm of San Francisco de Asís

and watching his sheep graze on a nearby hill. He could think only of all the good he would like to do in the world, if only by some miracle he were to be healed. Suddenly, from across the acequia, his patron saint, San Esquípulas, appeared and made a sign for him to come. Bernardo pushed aside his blankets and hobbled slowly toward the saint. But, due to his weakened condition, he was unable to get across the ditch before the apparition disappeared. He fell on his knees in the place where he had seen San Esquípulas and was instantly cured.

News travels fast in a tiny community, and soon everyone knew Don Bernardo had been healed. Others came and touched the dirt from the spot to their bodies, and they were also cured of their afflictions. Finally, in gratitude, a church to honor San Esquípulas was erected on that spot. Today a painting of the saint hangs prominently in the main reredos of Santuario. This exceptional work is attributed to Molleno (1804–1854?), "the chili painter"—a name given because some of his background foliage has the look of chili pods.

Through the years, another figure, Santo Niño de Atocha, has become increasingly important to the local residents and to the pilgrims who flock to Santuario. No one can quite explain the reason for this. His image stands on the main altar and is repeated in numerous places throughout the church; in the sacristy, he is celebrated in his own quaint shrine. If you ask local people or shopkeepers about Santo Niño, you might hear at least two popular stories.

In one, a man and his daughter were driving a yoke of oxen to the field when the child heard the sound of a campana, a church bell, coming out of the ground. She begged her father to stop and find it. He dug until he unearthed the bell; then, thinking he saw something else, he dug deeper and found the statue of Santo Niño de Atocha. Some people say that the spot producing the holy dirt is the same spot where Santo Niño was found.

Sacristy: Santo Niño de Atocha in a shrine with Big Bird sneakers, a worshiper's offering to the peripatetic Holy Child

The second story involves the San Ildefonso Indian potter, María Martínez. It seems she was seriously ill and her mother made a promise that if her daughter recovered she would make a pilgrimage to the Santuario. María took sacred dirt from the little chapel, rubbed herself with it, tasted it, and then prayed to the Holy Child that she would be healed. As the legend goes, Santo Niño appeared in the spot from which she took the holy dirt.

Santo Niño de Atocha is also sometimes called Santo Niño Perdido, because he is said to leave the chapel at night to walk through the country surrounding Chimayó. As a result of these nightly peregrinations, the little saint is constantly wearing out his shoes. Pilgrims to the shrine often bring new shoes in the smallest baby sizes for him. On my last trip to the shrine I saw that someone had left the saint a tiny pair of Big Bird sneakers.

During Holy Week, pilgrims walk for hundreds of miles along the highways toward Santuario, to converge on the little church and spend Good Friday in prayer, contemplation, and fellowship. Some make the painful trip on crutches or in wheelchairs; others, even less fortunate, are carried in the arms of parents or friends. Singly, in pairs, or in groups, they come out of sorrow, out of hope, and out of faith. They wait in long lines and file slowly into the church to pray and dig healing dirt from the *posito,* or hole, in the floor of the tiny room off the sacristy.

Good Friday is not without its tragedies. Pilgrims on the highways have been struck by automobiles and killed. I recall at least one knifing. And on the morning of Good Friday a couple of years back, I witnessed a bloody fistfight between two teenage girls, which had erupted over the fact that one girl had spent the night around one of the bonfires with the boyfriend of the other girl. It became a clawing, scuffling struggle that attracted two or three hundred people before the boyfriend finally managed to pull the girls apart.

NUESTRA SÉNORA
DEL SAGRADO ROSARIO (TRUCHAS)

Highway 76 rides the ridges of the hills up through the pinions at the base of the Sangre de Cristo Mountains to Truchas, a small village that seems precariously tacked onto the edge of the world. There is a cluster of crosses on the right, then a morada, a meetinghouse of the Penitente Brotherhood, on the left. The road narrows between Tafoya's Truchas General Store and the Exxon station. Glimpses of the church can be seen through the alleyways on the right-hand side. Nuestra Señora del Sagrado Rosario, the old church at Truchas, is sandwiched between houses, as though for protection. It faces east, looking beyond a house where a ruined Buick LeSabre rusts against a group of ancient rough-sawn wood buildings. Inside the low wall in front of the church is a blue-and-white cross, the horizontal member temporarily repaired with a piece of unpainted wood. The whole thing—cross, church, and wall—seems to lean with the weight of the single bell tower that rises on the right side.

The door opening into the sacristy on the south side of the building reveals a large, sturdy cabinet. Sitting on it is a beautiful but worn Santo Niño in a wooden niche.

With the exception of a green tinned ceiling over the sanctuary, the feeling of the interior of this church is similar to Córdova, only slightly simpler and more rustic.

Bulto of Jesús Nazareño at the front of the north side of the nave

The main reredos and various other paintings have not withstood time nearly so well, though the paintings in many of the panels are beautifully articulated, notably God the Father in the top row, Nuestra Señora del Rosario in the next one down, and San José and San Antonio in the bottom row. Flanking the reredos are bultos of San José on the left and Nuestra Señora del Rosario on the right, both draped in white; in the center is San José, also in white. There is a very handsome Jesús Nazareño at the front of the north side of the nave; the figure, in a robe of deep red, can just be seen through parted lace curtains.

Front view of Nuestra Señora del Sagrado Rosario in Truchas

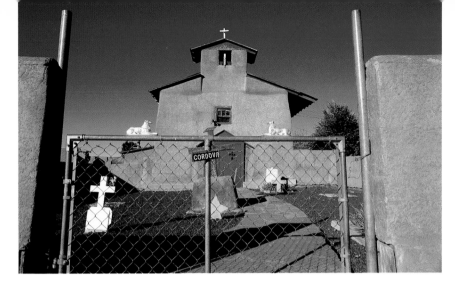

Front view of San Antonio de Padua del Pueblo Quemado, with gate

Nuestra Señora de Guadalupe depicted on a reredos leaning against north wall of the sanctuary

The three reredoses at San Antonio de Padua del Pueblo Quemado

Nuestra Señora del Rosario, north reredos

SAN ANTONIO DE
PADUA DEL PUEBLO QUEMADO (CÓRDOVA)

The sinuous State Highway 76, the High Road to Taos, winds slowly out of Española along the Santa Cruz River, up through Chimayó, and rises into the foothills of the Sangre de Cristos. The turnoff to Córdova drops quickly back down toward the river and gradually degenerates to a rutted dirt track. This picturesque village was the home of the artist José Rafael Aragón; his is a rich legacy and, partly because of it, Córdova is known as an important center for fine wood-carvers and artists who carry on the tradition.

From a distance, the cross on the top of the church bell tower is visible briefly against a quilt of corrugated tin roofs. Then it disappears, and one is left to find one's way to it through a labyrinth of narrow, potholed streets.

I first saw the church by accident. Driving through the streets, I came upon it from the back, its buttressed nave appearing like San Francisco at Ranchos de Taos, only smaller and lacking that church's impact. A narrow street circles the church and opens just enough to allow for a small number of parking spaces in front. The gate, of galvanized pipe and wire-mesh fencing, has two small silver-colored greyhounds decorating the top bar. Below them a tiny sign, hanging askew, reads: CÓRDOVA.

San Antonio de Padua del Pueblo Quemado is a small old parish church, visited for weekly Mass by one of the priests from Chimayó. Some time recently, the red wooden cross in front of the building seems to have been broken from its concrete base and then wedged back into the hole, but at a tilt. The church contains a magnificent collection of the art of José Rafael Aragón, who, according to the records in the Santa Cruz church, was

first buried here. In the 1867 inventory of Santa Cruz de la Cañada, Father Juan de Jesús Trujillo recorded: "Two sculptured statues of Our Lady of Carmel, one of them made during my time by the sculptor Rafael Aragón who in turn would be paid for with his burial." And, perhaps for that reason, the artist was reburied at Santa Cruz. For, as Father Trujillo wrote in the burial records: "With regard to the burial record of the late Rafael Aragón, it is true he was buried in the Chapel of St. Anthony of Quemado [now Córdova], but after laying him to rest, it was determined to bring the body to the parish church, Santa Cruz de la Cañada, and he was buried in the Chapel of Our Lady of Carmel with an elaborate funeral and because it is true, I sign it on the same day, Juan de Jesús Trujillo."

Crowded into the sanctuary are three reredoses, a large main one in the center, on which there are thirteen painted panels with the Holy Spirit as a dove at top center; eight bultos either hang from this reredos or stand in front of it. Leaning against the walls on either side of the sanctuary are two smaller reredoses. There are five very fine bultos arranged along the bottom of the reredos against the south wall. In the left niche is Nuestra Señora de los Dolores, in white; in the large center

niche are Nuestra Señora del Rosario, Nuestra Señora de los Dolores (showing the seven sorrows), and San José con el Niño; in the right niche is Nuestra Señora de los Dolores, in black. In the niches of the north reredos are four more extraordinary bultos: Nuestra Señora de Guadalupe, Nuestra Señora del Rosario, San Miguel, and the Santo Niño in a chair.

Sometimes the garish additions in churches have their own charm, sometimes they are merely appalling. In Córdova, when I was last there, I saw fastened to the reredos that leans against the south side of the sanctuary wall a brand-new, bright-red fire extinguisher. I hated it at first as much as if it had been affixed to a Picasso. But as I thought about it, I realized that it told me something I had not known about the people who worship in Córdova, the people who have kept this church repaired and functioning.

Mercifully, little beyond the addition of the fire extinguisher has been done to change the church. Out of the public eye, serving as a chapel for pious village people, it had survived with only the natural additions of time and a few cheap plaster figures that serve to point up the incredibly beautiful work in the real bultos and paintings.

Detail of south reredos: Nuestra Señora de los Dolores and fire extinguisher

59

San José at Las Trampas is distinctly different from most of the other churches in northern New Mexico. Although once probably the focal point of a traditional plaza for Santo Tomás Apóstol del Rio de las Trampas—as the village was established in 1751—the church now stands virtually alone on a rise overlooking the remnants of that early plaza. There is about the building an openness and a feeling of solid mass that reflects the fortitude of the poor mountain people who built it.

The nave

Detail of east reredos

After Bishop Pedro Tamarón visited Las Trampas in 1760 and gave permission for the construction of a church 30 varas (about 82½ feet) in length, the community began to canvass for funds. Sixteen years later, in the brief section of his report concerning Las Trampas, Fray Francisco Atanasio Domínguez wrote that chief among the members of the little community who went out seeking contributions was the patriarch Juan de Argüello, a man in his eighties. Argüello and his people were tireless in their efforts and found enough money to begin work on the building.

Like Santa Cruz, San José is laid out in the shape of a cross, giving space for multiple altars. There are two unmatched towers at the front of the church and a balcony between them that can be reached from the choir loft. The raw, hand-rubbed adobe, burred with fine straw, has been smoothed down by the faithful of the village. Periodically, when the adobe is in need of repair, they gather and apply a new coat, troweling it on and smoothing it down with their bare hands and pieces of sheepskin. For these people, the old church has always been an object of love; their work for its preservation is like the laying on of hands, the people blessing the church that blesses them.

On the inside San José is even more stunning. It seems the least adulterated of the New Mexican churches, ranking with San Xavier del Bac, the great Kino church southwest of Tucson, Arizona. Once the door creaks open on its ancient hinges, one sees the heavy plank floors worn from centuries of use, the unmatched benches, two facing reredoses, and the painted stations of the cross. The magnificent reredos behind the main altar and many of the other paintings have been attributed to Pedro Antonio Fresquis, recognized as the first santero born in New Mexico (1749). He spent his early years in Santa Cruz and later moved to Las Trampas. In the mid-nineteenth century, the main reredos was repainted by Pedro Gonzales, an itinerant Mexican workman, whose more garish colors have gradually softened with age. Now there is about them a rich, glowing quality as they are touched by light from the clerestory panes above the transept.

San José is a noble structure that deserves celebration. It is one of approximately a dozen churches built in the eighteenth century or earlier that still remain standing. In its line, its mass, and the sheer beauty of its art, it is the embodiment of all that the adobe church was meant to be.

SAN FRANCISCO DE ASÍS
DE LAS TRAMPAS DE RANCHOS DE TAOS

Every area in the Southwest has one special church or mission that has received national attention, often for reasons having little to do with religion. In Texas, it is the abandoned mission San Antonio de Valero, which became famous as the Alamo. San Juan Capistrano in Southern California is probably better known for its returning swallows than for any of its remarkable mission history. In New Mexico, San Francisco de Asís de las Trampas de Ranchos de Taos has the distinction of having been

Rear view of the sculptured walls and buttresses of San Francisco de Asís de las Trampas de Ranchos de Taos. This spectacular church has been sketched, painted, and photographed by more famous American artists than perhaps any other single building in the United States.

From the northwest side

Ranchos de Taos, from the front

Detail of the north reredos, painted by Molleno, the "chili painter," featuring Nuestro Señor de Esquípulas

the subject of more works of art by more famous artists than any other single structure in the state—possibly in the United States.

Since it was completed in 1815, San Francisco has commanded the attention of traveler as well as artist. Its massive transept, most often seen from the rear, is startlingly sculptural, composed of soft, flowing lines that seem almost capriciously drawn—though they are, as with the huge rounded corner buttresses, both functional and essential. As a monumental form, San Francisco seems to change continually, magically, in the play of light and shadow.

Inside, the church is illuminated by two large arched windows, a departure from the old fortress style. A finely carved San Francisco, holding skull and cross, stands in the central niche of the main reredos. Around this bulto are eight panels of paintings. The moldings and the small twisting columns are hand-carved, held together by wooden pegs. To the right of the transept is a large reredos by Molleno, "the chili painter." The focus piece in this altar is the crucifix, Nuestro Señor de Esquípulas, a version of which also hangs in the main reredos at El Santuario in Chimayó. There are four other bultos and eight painted panels.

Like its exterior, the interior of San Francisco is irregular. The nave is intersected by a transept that forms a kind of leaning cross; from the south end of the transept a door leads to the sacristy in which there is a fine old painting of the Mother and Child. The nave measures approximately eighty-five feet long by twenty-five feet wide, and rises to twenty-five feet at the ceiling. However, no measurement in inches or feet—or in the old Spanish varas—can describe the elegance and grace of this church, inside and out.

From the south side

SAN AGUSTÍN DE LA ISLETA

There is an amazing legend that concerns the Isleta church. Fray Juan Padilla, one of the priests who traveled with Coronado and was later martyred, is said to have been buried in the sanctuary of the church. When his mummified remains were brought to San Agustín, from the cave in which they had lain for nearly two centuries, they were buried in a coffin made from the trunk of a hollowed-out cottonwood tree.

The father, however, refused to stay in his grave. Periodically—some say every year, others every generation, usually when an epidemic illness or something of that nature occurs—Fray Padilla, in his cottonwood coffin, makes his way to the surface and reveals his remains to the people. They are examined by the faithful of the pueblo—bits of his clothing have been kept as treasured relics and used in a number of miraculous healings and cures—and then he is reburied. The church and others have launched investigations to discredit the story. Nevertheless, pe-

Small altar at San Agustín: The costumes worn by the virgin and the figure in the unusual cruciform painting are typical of the Indian style, which dominates this old mission church.

The massive facade of San Agustín de la Isleta

72

riodically, a body is found in the cottonwood coffin, examined, and reburied. In the process, Fray Padilla has become a saint—at least to the local people.

San Agustín de la Isleta, where the martyred priest is supposedly still buried—however unquietly—is a large, solidly buttressed building at the north end of the public plaza near the center of the Isleta pueblo. This Tewa village is located on the banks of the Rio Grande about thirteen miles south of Albuquerque, off Interstate 25. The name Isleta, "little island," is descriptive, dating back to a spring flood season when the swollen Rio Grande spread until its waters surrounded the high ground upon which the village was built.

The original church, portions of which make up the present structure, was erected about 1613. Like most of the great New Mexican churches, San Agustín has had a turbulent history, much of which has been reflected in changes to its facade over the centuries. In 1776, Fray Atanasio Domínguez recorded that it had a "two-leaved door three varas high" (a little over eight feet) with turrets on the two front corners. Ninety years later those turrets were gone, and above the double front door and large mullioned window was a small open belfry in which hung a single bell. A photograph taken in 1881 shows that the belfry had given way to two enclosed wooden bell towers, each designed like the steeple of a New England church. By the early twentieth century, the twin towers had been altered again and embellished until they consisted of two large spires, each surrounded by four small spires, and all crowned with wooden crosses. The effect was comic. But it was not unusual. During this period, similar treatment was given to other churches in New Mexico and to some mission churches in the California chain. The gingerbread was finally removed from San Agustín in a major remodeling undertaken in 1959; when that was completed the following year, the San Agustín facade looked much as it does today: massive and firm, with two towers, a small belfry in the center, and a smaller bell hanging just above the entranceway.

Isleta and its reflection

SAN FELIPE NERI

Exterior of San Felipe Neri

San Felipe Neri, the sixteenth-century Florentine saint for whom the unusual Albuquerque church is named, was known as a fastidious man who carefully avoided religious dispute. By contrast, San Felipe Neri, the church, has endured a long history of controversy, which continues up to the present time.

Located on the plaza in Old Town and surrounded by a crush of restaurants and shops aimed primarily at the tourist trade, San Felipe is the replacement for the original church of that name, which collapsed in 1793. Following a decree by Governor Fernando de la Concha, in which he admonished the citizens to support the project, a new building was erected on the plaza. That basic structure, put up nearly two centuries ago, forms the heart of the present church.

San Felipe Neri is a curious combination of architectural styles. It began as an adobe church in the traditional New Mexi-

Nuestra Señora de Guadalupe: detail of a carving in one of the trees in the parking lot behind San Felipe Neri, Albuquerque

Facade of San Felipe Neri, showing the controversial stonework

can style, functionally simple and direct. But its caretakers have been priests of amazingly diverse cultural backgrounds and tastes—Spanish, Mexican, New Mexican, French, and Italian—and each, it seems, has left his personal mark on the church.

During the 1850s, San Felipe was redecorated under the supervision of Father Joseph Machebeuf, one of the French priests brought into New Mexico by Bishop Lamy. There followed a gradual but relentless transformation that would in time cover up more and more of the New Mexican character of this church. One major move, also seen at Isleta and other places, was the addition of ornate Victorian bell towers. In 1868, Italian Jesuit priests came to San Felipe, and there began another era of change, this largely confined to the interior. The ceiling was tinned, covering the traditional vigas and corbels; woodwork not characteristic of the adobe church was added; and trompe l'oeil painting was applied to give various surfaces the appearance of polished marble.

There may be no end to such changes. Perhaps the destiny of San Felipe Neri is one of perpetual alteration, each new remodeling taking it further from its simple beginnings. As late as 1978, more additions were being made to the church. In that year, under the direction of Father George Salazar, a veneer of artificial stone was applied to portions of the building, giving it the look of a large suburban ranch-style house. Father Salazar was cited for an infraction against a city ordinance protecting landmarks. He went to court, where the judge ruled the ordinance unconstitutional. Father Salazar may have won his case, but it was a loss to history and to anyone concerned with the preservation of important architectural monuments.

SAN MIGUEL

San Miguel, the "little chapel" on the south side of the Santa Fe River

San Miguel has always been the little chapel on the south side of the Santa Fe River. The first church on this site was built in 1621 to serve the Indians who had been brought from Mexico to New Mexico to work as servants and laborers. That building was torn down in 1640; it was reconstructed, and the new church was subsequently torched during the 1680 Pueblo Revolt. Only its walls remained when the Spaniards reconquered New Mexico and returned to Santa Fe.

In 1693, there was a plan to rebuild San Miguel, but no conclusive evidence exists that anything was actually done until 1710. In fact, a study conducted in 1955 by Stanley Stubbs and Bruce Ellis of the Laboratory of Anthropology at Santa Fe, during which the adobe walls, timbers, and flooring of the chapel were examined, indicates that much of the present structure was probably built in 1709–10. The study corroborates the words carved on a timber in the choir loft: *El Señor Marquéz de la Peñuela Hizo esta fábrica alferes Rl Dn Agn flos Vergara su criado Año de 1710.* ("The Marqués de la Peñuela made this building with the help of Alferes Real Don Agustín Flores Vergara, his servant, in the year 1710.")

Since that time, the exterior of San Miguel has undergone considerable change. At one point, the church had twin towers. Added at a later date was a tall tower with at least three belfries. That tower collapsed and was replaced by a large, squarish, open tower surmounted by a wooden cross of stark white.

Among the artifacts inside San Miguel is the striking reredos—possibly the work of the santero known as the Laguna Painter—which was cleaned and restored in 1955 by E. Boyd, the eminent scholar and conservator of Spanish colonial art. The panel, dated 1798 and bearing an inscription announcing that it had been donated to the church by Antonio José Ortiz, contains a number of important paintings. At the top center is San Miguel. Below that is a painting of Christ with an elaborately painted border. Of the four oval paintings, at the top left is a portrait of Santa Teresa de Jesús, and, top right, is Santa Gertrudis; on the lower left is San Francisco de Asís, and on the right is San Luis Rey de Francia.

San Miguel's proportions—it is approximately seventy-five feet long, twenty-four feet wide, and twenty-five feet high—are ample proof of the success of the early Franciscans' attempts at taking a simple structure, the single fortresslike nave, adding an extra measure of height, and admitting light to invoke feelings of peace and piety.

The reredos behind the altar at San Miguel, possibly the work of the Laguna Painter

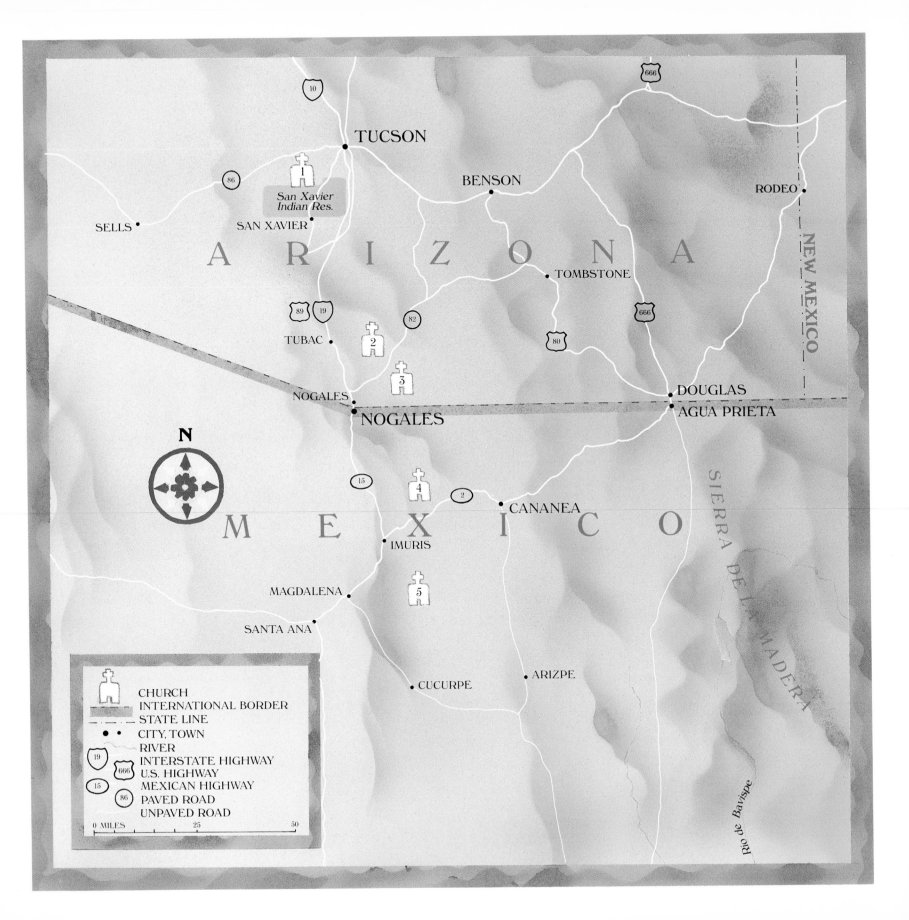

TUCSON

BENSON

RODEO

SELLS

SAN XAVIER

San Xavier
Indian Res.

1

A R I Z O N A

TOMBSTONE

NEW MEXICO

89 19

TUBAC

2

82

666

80

DOUGLAS

3

NOGALES

NOGALES

AGUA PRIETA

N

15

4

2

CANANEA

M E X I C O

IMURIS

SIERRA DE LA MADERA

MAGDALENA

5

SANTA ANA

CUCURPE

ARIZPE

Rio de Bavispe

CHURCH
INTERNATIONAL BORDER
STATE LINE
CITY, TOWN
RIVER
INTERSTATE HIGHWAY
U.S. HIGHWAY
MEXICAN HIGHWAY
PAVED ROAD
UNPAVED ROAD

19

666

15

86

0 MILES   25   50

PADRE EUSEBIO FRANCISCO KINO

The early history of the Pimeria Alta, an area that reaches northward from what is now the state of Sonora in Mexico to the Gila River in present-day Arizona, is dominated by the deeds of one amazing man. Indeed, Padre Eusebio Francisco Kino is probably the most remarkable individual to have worked the Spanish frontier in the New World. Although the monuments built under his guidance are among the most beautiful examples of religious architecture in the Southwest, it is for his spirit and his indefatigable zeal as explorer, missionary, and borderland ambassador that he is best remembered. The churches are only tokens of the greatness of his deeds.

Eusebio Kino was born in 1645 in Segno, Italy, a small mountain town near the Italian Alps. His studies eventually took him to a Jesuit college in Austria, where he almost died from a serious illness. He promised his patron saint, St. Francis Xavier, that if he were given back his good health he would join the Jesuits.

As he continued to study and distinguish himself in the fields of astronomy, mathematics, and cartography, Kino dreamed of a mission in China. Instead, he was sent to serve in Mexico —though it took the eager young missionary an inordinate length of time to reach his new post. Circumstances caused him to miss his first ship, and he was forced to wait two years for the next one, which promptly ran aground as it sailed out of the Bay of Cádiz. Six months later he found passage on another vessel, and after three months at sea he landed in the port city of Vera Cruz.

When an expedition was being formed in Mexico to colonize Baja California, Admiral Isidro Atondo enlisted Kino in the capacity of royal cartographer as well as missionary. California captured the imagination of Kino. With many other Spaniards, he at first viewed it as a huge island—a theory he himself would disprove many years later.

In spite of Padre Kino's enthusiastic efforts at reaching out to the Indians with his kindness and Christianity, Atondo's attempt at establishing a permanent colony in Baja proved no more successful than had earlier ones. The Indians might have gotten on with Kino, but not with the Spanish soldiers, whose methods were brutal and unfeeling. In the face of growing Indian hostility, the colonists finally fled to La Paz.

Later that year, 1683, Kino accompanied Admiral Atondo as he sailed from San Lucas, a more northerly point along the coast, to San Bruno, where they established a new colony. From there,

The ruin of Nuestra Señora del Pilar y Santiago de Cocospera, Sonora, Mexico

Kino crossed the Cerro de Giganta Mountains and found his way to the Pacific Ocean. But Baja was a hard, uncompromising land, and drought and disease steadily took their toll on the colonists and soldiers. So Atondo pulled out of Baja California, taking with him the reluctant Father Kino.

While he was preparing to take up his next assignment, which was to establish a mission on the Sea of Cortéz among the Seri Indians, Kino turned his energies toward a problem he had grown increasingly concerned about: the exploitation of the Indians in the mines of Mexico. He discussed the situation with the Royal Audiencia in Guadalajara and obtained a copy of a royal cédula, a decree made by Carlos II, freeing the Indians from forced labor for a period of twenty years. He lost little time in circulating this document through the missions and bringing it to the attention of other authorities. Such was the spirit that animated Kino as he rode north to explore new frontiers and pioneer new missions.

Unlike some other frontier missions, those Kino established held no Indians in bondage; they were free to work or not. Rather than compel them to Christianity, Kino tried to make his faith attractive to them—and this he did in part by the example of his own life. He was uncommon in his ideas about how religion should work. He took his faith outside the church and made it a part of the everyday life of the people he served. He seemed to see no dichotomy between the spiritual and material needs of his people and he worked hard to serve both.

Father Kino never reached his post among the Seri Indians. Mañuel Gonzáles, the father visitor of Sonora, called on him to begin opening up the territory inhabited by the Pimas Altas. This was—and, in some ways, still is—a brutal and unforgiving country.

His first move was to establish a center of operations at Cosari, which he called Nuestra Señora de los Dolores de Cosari. The building of Dolores was the beginning of a long burst of creative energy directed toward reshaping the social and economic structure of the entire Pimeria Alta area. Kino taught the Indian farmers, who had been working their land for generations, how to increase their production, gave them new crops to grow, and helped them build ranches for cattle, sheep, and goats.

He went about his work with a tireless zeal, and word of his successes reached the top levels of the mission administration and were then relayed to the Jesuit general, head of the Society of Jesus in Rome. But Kino was not without his enemies and detractors. His was the kind of success that breeds jealousy in lesser men, who criticized his aggressive missionary conduct as unseemly for a man of God.

Father Juan María Salvatierra was sent in 1690 as a visitor general to weigh the truth against the accusations and determine if Kino's mission should be closed. Contrary to what he had feared, Father Salvatierra discovered prospering mission villages full of Indians who seemed genuinely touched by the spirit of Kino.

During these early years, Father Kino left an important architectural legacy in the Pimeria Alta. Nothing remains of Nuestra

85

Señora de los Dolores or Nuestra Señora de los Remedios; only a crumbling ruin stands of Nuestra Señora del Pilar y Santiago de Cocospera and even less of Los Santos Ángeles de Guevarí. Of the churches that do remain, many have been rebuilt or refurbished, but they continue as remarkable monuments to Father Kino. There are San Ignacio de Caburica, San Pedro y San Pablo del Tubutama, San Antonio del Oquitoa, San Diego del Pitiquito, La Purísima Concepción de Nuestra Señora de Caborca, San Cayetano del Tumacacori, and San Xavier del Bac. Of these only Tumacacori and San Xavier are in the United States.

Unremitting in his efforts at bringing about peaceful coexistence among the tribes living in his high-desert outpost, Kino was able to forge an alliance among the Piman people that served effectively against the encroachment of the neighboring Apaches and Jocomes. It was part of his strategy for gradually opening the way to expansion into California, a desire he had had since his early disappointing experiences with the Atondo expeditions.

He threaded his way through the Pimeria Alta, crisscrossing the landscape, climbing its peaks and exploring its valleys, tracing its shape on his intricate and amazingly accurate maps. Through the years his desire to know more about the country impelled him to undertake various expeditions that eventually made it clear to him that California was not an island, as he and everyone else had thought. Kino was no mere dreamer, however; each entrada, each grueling pack trip, into the new country to the north enlarged the number of people whose lives he touched and added new meaning to his mission.

After climbing El Nazareño, a peak in the desert, and seeing the mountains of California, Father Kino was convinced it could be reached by boat. He had no boat, so he began building one at Caborca, over a hundred miles from the Gulf of California. In his usual style, he started stockpiling various kinds of wood and set about making plans. But his boat was never to be built. The project was halted by the father visitor, Juan Muñoz de Burgos.

In 1695, Father Francisco Xavier Saeta was assigned to Caborca, and Father Kino was instructed to supply him with all he might need to establish his mission. Father Saeta had made a fine start at Caborca when the mission became the center of a controversy fired by the medicine men and others who felt that the priests were usurping their powers. They went on a rampage, burning and destroying crops and buildings, and ended by martyring Father Saeta.

The Spanish cavalry arrived, and Kino set up a meeting between them and the Indian chiefs. The negotiations were pro-

San Xavier del Bac bell tower
and dome seen through the
rear gateway

San Xavier del Bac seen from
the northeast corner

Sculptural detail of San Xavier wall trim and bell tower

ceeding peacefully, if cautiously, until one of the perpetrators of the revolt was identified. Captain Antonio Solís thereupon drew his sword and summarily cut off the Indian's head. Certain they were in for the same fate, the assembled Indians ran for their lives. The soldiers opened fire, cutting down the innocent with the guilty.

War raged during the following few months. When the cavalry conceded it was unable to bring the Indians into submission, the soldiers pulled out and turned the situation over to Kino. It took him only a few days to put together the pieces and begin the process of rebuilding the peace that had existed before.

Once this was done he resumed his efforts at moving into

Detail of balcony and intricate plaster scrollwork

California. He rode to Mexico City to present a proposal he had worked out with Father Salvatierra, which outlined their plan to go to California without financial backing from the royal treasury. The proposal was accepted and Kino was assigned to move on to California.

But suddenly there was serious concern over what would happen to the Pimeria Alta without Kino. Kino himself came up with a solution, which he submitted to the father general in Rome. He suggested that he be allowed to split the year between California and Pimeria Alta. Accordingly, he was reinstated at Dolores, news of which prompted a celebration among the grateful Indians.

Kino was a unique Christian activist; he believed his work needed to be done, and he sometimes chose extravagant means of doing it. He organized a pilgrimage of the hundreds of Indians who had converged on Dolores to welcome him back. The procession he assembled made its way south through Arispe, Oposura, and Guasavas, ending in Bazeraca for an audience with Father Horacio Polici, the visitor general. Their point was made: they were promised more priests for instruction and soldiers to help defend the boundaries of their lands.

From this time on, Kino and his various companions—priests and soldiers and Indians—pressed the Spanish boundaries farther north and west. Late in 1697, Kino led an expedition that left Dolores, passed through the settlements of Cocospera and Suamca, and continued to Santa Cruz de Gaybanipitea. They went to Quiburí and met with Coro, chief of the Sobaipuri Indians; then Coro and a band of his men traveled with the Kino party along the San Pedro River to where it joins with the Gila. They swung west and found the ruins of Casa Grande, once a large and apparently prosperous settlement that had been reached inexplicably. Their farthest point in that trek was San Andrés. From there they turned to the Santa Cruz River and returned to Dolores.

During a good part of the next year, Father Kino was besieged with illness. In November, he took a small party back to San Andrés and circled down to Sonoyta. Traveling almost directly west of Sonoyta, Kino climbed Cerro de Santa Clara, which is today known as Pinacate Peak, and discovered that the Gulf of California extended much farther north than he had anticipated. Once again he altered his maps.

Three months later, in 1699, he was assembling people and supplies for another expedition. From Sonoyta, they set out on the treacherous Camino del Diablo and made their way to the

View showing the
unfinished bell tower

Gila River. Lieutenant Juan Mateo Manje, who had accompanied Kino on other expeditions, rode to a peak and made the discovery that the Gila did not empty into the Gulf of California, as they had assumed; rather, it flowed into the Colorado, a huge river by comparison, and the Colorado ran to the gulf.

Already in his mid-fifties, an age when most of his peers were content to move at a far slower pace, merely tending their missions, Father Kino kept advancing. He was, indeed, a whirlwind. On every side he saw something new that needed doing, that demanded his attention. The Order supported him, though they never sent enough priests. Father Salvatierra's Loretto Mission in California was struggling to hold its own; the missions and rancherias farther north needed servicing. To make that work easier, Kino decided to create a mission at Bac near present-day Tucson. In 1700 he set the cornerstones for a modest church that eventually grew into the magnificent San Xavier del Bac.

On the expedition to the lower Gila, the Yumán people had given Kino a handful of blue shells. Later, at Remedios, one of the chiefs from the Gila area presented him with a cross strung on a string with twenty of these blue abalone shells. Kino knew they had not come from the gulf. He had seen them once before, when he had made his way across Baja California to the Pacific. Now they could tell him something else. He set out to find the source of the shells, but the expedition had to be halted because of a rumor of Indian trouble. Meeting with a number of chiefs at San Xavier del Bac, he was able to piece together enough information to deduce that the shells had come as trade items in a series of transactions that brought them gradually overland from the Pacific. And with this information he established conclusively that California was not the island that people had long thought it was.

His mission was one of constant discovery, and he kept on the move until the very day of his death. He was always mounting up and riding out of Dolores or riding wearily back to recuperate for his next trip. In March of 1711, at the age of sixty-five, he rode to Magdalena to say a Mass of dedication for the St. Francis Xavier chapel. He was overcome during the Mass and

San Xavier toward sunset

Campanario

had to be carried to the priest's house, where he died on March 15, leaving a legacy that even today continues to grow.

The Kino churches, many of which have been rebuilt since his death, contain only small fragments of the original structures raised under his guidance. In the United States, there are three —San Xavier del Bac, the great baroque monument on the San Xavier Indian Reservation southwest of Tucson, San José de Tumacacori (originally San Cayetano del Tumacacori), protected as a national monument between Tucson and Nogales, and the ruins of Los Santos Ángeles de Guevarí, the earliest Jesuit mission in Arizona. Across the Mexican border in Sonora are a number of churches on sites chosen by Kino. The ruins of the once-elegant Nuestra Señora del Pilar y Santiago de Cocospera stand on a hill overlooking the Cocospera Valley between Imuris and Cananea. San Ignacio de Caburica is on the plaza of the sleepy village of San Ignacio, a few miles north of Magdalena. Almost directly west of Caburica, on the Altar River, is San Pedro y San Pablo del Tubutama, a striking eighteenth-century church erected where the early Kino chapel had stood. La Purísima Concepción de Nuestra Señora de Caborca, built in the early nineteenth century, is famous as the scene of two martyrdoms as well as the place where a force of American soldiers was executed. These churches, with a number of smaller chapels in the villages between them, are living monuments to help remember the efforts of Father Eusebio Francisco Kino.

CHURCHES
OF
TEXAS

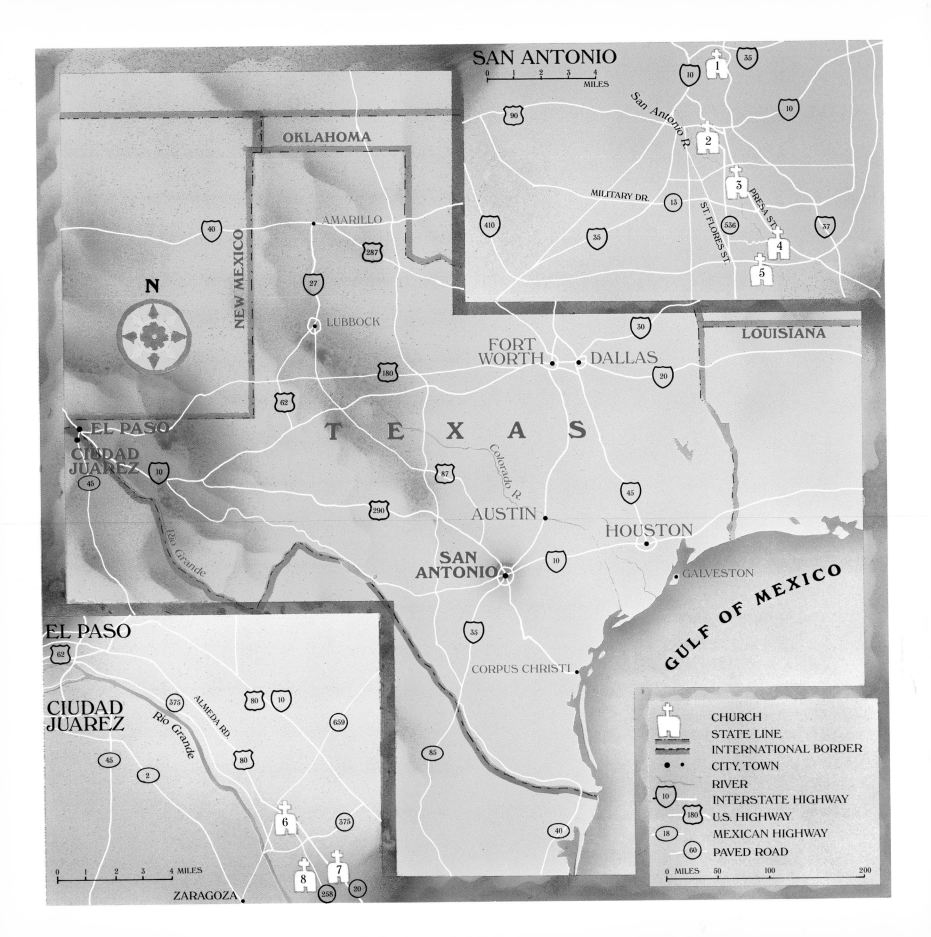

Captain Álvarez de Pineda, with four ships under his command, sailed out from Jamaica in 1519 and mapped the coast from Florida to Vera Cruz in Mexico; he noted the mouths of the Mississippi and Rio Grande and claimed for the Spanish crown the territory later known as Texas. Aside from numerous explorations, little else was done to colonize Texas for almost two centuries. Then, with threats of invasion and economic expansion through the aggressive acts of two French explorers, La Salle and, later, St. Denis, the Spanish began to act.

Governor Alonso de León, accompanied by Father Damian Massanet, three other Franciscan friars, and over one hundred armed troops, dedicated the first East Texas mission, San Francisco, on the west side of the Neches River in 1690; it was abandoned some two years later. On July 3, 1716, Captain Domingo Ramón again took possession of Texas for the Spanish crown. He established during the next few weeks, in addition to fortresses, or presidios, four missions in East Texas—San Francisco de los Tejas, Nuestra Señora de la Purísima Concepción de los Hasani, Nuestra Señora de Guadalupe, and San José de los Nazonis. Two more missions, San Miguel de Linares and Nuestra Señora de los Dolores, were added in the fall of that year. And two more were built the following year. But the French continued to be a worrisome factor, and it became apparent that if the Spanish intended to continue to occupy the area they would need additional military support to do so.

Father Antonio de San Buenaventura Olivares presented a plan to the viceroy in Mexico City in which he outlined a way to strengthen the East Texas missions and establish new, more effective missions on the Río San Antonio. The viceroy was attracted to Father Olivares's idea and accepted it, designating Don Martín de Alarcón, the recently appointed governor of Coahuila, as captain general and governor of Texas, thus empowering him to oversee the venture. Father Olivares was placed in charge of creating the new missions, and after a lengthy delay brought

about in part by a disagreement between Alarcón and Olivares, the founding of San Antonio de Valero, the first mission in the San Antonio area, took place on May 1, 1718.

Alarcón went on to assess the Spanish holdings in East Texas. His findings were disappointing. Sickness, which felled Alarcón himself and others in his party, had badly crippled the missions. Added to the ever-increasing presence of the French, this made maintaining the missions a serious liability. The situation never improved, and the East Texas missions were shut down and eventually relocated to the Río San Antonio.

Keystone detail from the Alamo

NUESTRA SEÑORA
DE LA PURÍSIMA CONCEPCIÓN DE ACUÑA

When Nuestra Señora de la Purísima Concepción de los Hasani was officially moved from East Texas to San Antonio, its name was changed to de Acuña, in honor of the viceroy of New Spain and Marqués de Casafuerte, Juan de Acuña. Here, the mission would finally flourish, and its church would be a credit to anyone's name.

Concepción is thought to be the oldest church still in use as a church in the state of Texas. Some people say, too, that it is the oldest unrestored stone church in the United States. Whether those claims are true or not, Concepción is an extraordinarily beautiful building. Its architecture, a vaulted cruciform with a dome where the arms intersect, is sophisticated and well proportioned. Unlike so many churches whose bell towers appear to have been an afterthought or are the objects of constant change, the towers of Concepción are integral to the mass of the building; be-

107

Misión Nuestra Señora de la
Purísima Concepción de Acuña,
with ruins in the foreground

neath them are two small vaulted chapels, whose once-splendid wall paintings have deteriorated until little of their former beauty remains. The generously proportioned cupola, or dome, finished at the top with narrow panes of glass in a circular lantern, offsets the weight of the towers and adds unity to the design.

Dedicated December 8, 1755, this magnificent church took twenty years to build. The blocks of light-colored, porous limestone were cut from a quarry a short distance away, which also supplied the stone for other missions along the San Antonio. The solid craftsmanship that went into Concepción is apparent even from a distance. Only upon closer inspection does one detect the flaws that have resulted from vandalism and neglect.

Perhaps because of its spare, relatively sophisticated stonework, Concepción seems far more Spanish than many of the adobe structures in other areas of the Southwest. There is also a Moorish influence evident in the buttressed exterior walls, the dome, and the blunt, spirelike forms that line the capstone.

The design of the facade is simple but commanding. Carved into the lintel at the top of the doorway is the Spanish inscription: *A Su Patrona Y Princesa Con Estas Armas Atiende Esta Misión, Y Defiende El Punto De Su Pureza* ("To its Patroness and Princess, with these arms this mission serves and protects the point [doctrine] of her purity"). Above this and to the left is a carving of the Franciscan arms—the left arm of Jesus crossing over the right arm of St. Francis and both nailed to a cross—and above to the right are the five wounds of Jesus and the twelve knots, more important imagery of the Franciscan Order.

William Corner, writing in 1890, described an aspect of the facade that today is no longer evident: "The front of Concepción must have been very gorgeous with color, for it was frescoes all over with red and blue quatrefoil crosses and with large yellow and orange squares to simulate dressed stones. This frescoing is rapidly disappearing."

The most beautiful room inside the church is the baptistery, located to the right of the front door. There is a fine carved stone font, and on the wall above it is an intriguing, though badly deteriorated, painting of the crucifixion. Other patchy fragments of wall painting remain around the room, though they have been sadly defaced by the scratching and scribbling of visitors and vandals. Further examples of the original eighteenth-century painting can be seen in the small room, opposite the baptistery, from which the bell was rung, as well as in rooms that apparently served as living quarters for the priests.

SAN JOSÉ Y SAN MIGUEL DE AGUAYO

Facade detail: San José, with Holy Infant, stands above the round window; San Francisco de Asís is to the right, and Santa Domingo is to the left.

Bell tower and dome of San José seen beyond the original mission wall

The majestic San José y San Miguel de Aguayo church, still inside the walls of the mission, was begun in 1768, when Father Gaspar José de Solís and Governor Hugo de Oconor laid the cornerstones, and was completed in 1782. Unlike Concepción, much of San José y San Miguel de Aguayo was damaged during the years after secularization and continued to deteriorate until it was rebuilt in the 1930s. The facade, with its intricately carved stonework, is much more reminiscent of European churches than those of the Spanish frontier in the New World. Fortunately, the facade as well as the famous rose window are mostly original. Parts of them were damaged by U.S. Army soldiers stationed at the mission in the 1840s, who used them for target practice; but these have been carefully restored.

The brilliant carved stone of the facade and the rose window at San José has been attributed to Pedro Huizar. Widely circulated romantic stories about Huizar, which depicted him as a lovesick Spaniard separated from his sweetheart and pining for her while he chipped away at his glorious window and lived the life of a celibate, have been largely discredited. Huizar was apparently a Mexican, born in Aguascalientes, who lived at the mission with his wife and worked on the stones with the single-minded devotion of a true artisan.

The beautifully articulated facade of the church has been noted by many critics. Even Father Juan Agustín Morfi, known to be less than generous in his criticism of the frontier churches, was favorably impressed: "The facade is very costly because of the statues and ornaments with which it was heavily decorated, detracting somewhat from its natural beauty. . . . In a word, no one could have imagined that there were such good artists in so desolate a place." San José, holding the Holy Infant, stands above the large round window. To his right is San Francisco, skull in one hand, a cross in the other; the figure on the left, with a book, is Santo Domingo. Below the round window and directly above the doorway is the Virgen de Guadalupe. To the right of the door is Santa Ana, a child in her arms; the figure on the left is probably San Joaquín. Worked into the intricate carving of the facade are cherubim, the Sacred Heart, shells, foliage, and various other designs created to accommodate the major imagery and hold it together in a rich artistic texture.

The intricate rose window that looks out from the sacristy is a wonder, almost out of place in this outpost of civilization in which hand-building just an ordinary structure was sometimes

Ruins of the once-elaborate Misión San José

Misión San José: the sacristy altar consecrated to the Virgen de Guadalupe

Stone portals from the mission ruins behind the sacristy

as difficult as the business of simply staying alive.

After the elegance of the exterior, the interior of the nave is anticlimactic. The sacristy itself is more arresting, as it contains a number of fine bultos and a much-used altar consecrated to the Virgen de Guadalupe.

Situated in the ruins of what appears to have been a fabulous mission, San José gives the visitor a more complete view of the contrasts of life on the Río San Antonio than its famous companion mission, San Antonio de Valero, known today as the Alamo. Aside from the church, there are a number of other mission buildings, some restored and others in ruin, that provide a look at the complexity and scope of mission life. While the church was central to the mission, it was more than anything else a political institution, dealing in all aspects of frontier life. As at San José, the successful mission was a complete spiritual, economic, and governmental unit.

SAN JUAN CAPISTRANO

After the grandly proportioned La Purísima Concepción and San José, San Juan Capistrano, located farther south along the Río San Antonio, seems small and slightly insignificant. Constructed in the mid-eighteenth century, it was meant to be replaced by a larger and much grander church. That building was begun but never finished. Only fragments of it remain, in a ruin that lies to the east across a grassy quadrangle.

As with the other Texas missions, the history of San Juan Capistrano is underscored by problems and change. First established in East Texas as San José de los Nazonis in July 1716, it was moved to the Colorado River near present-day Austin, and then, on March 5, 1731, it was relocated in San Antonio and renamed San Juan Capistrano to avoid confusion with San José y san Miguel de Aguayo.

The small church is entered by a side door through one of the Roman arches that create the building's simple design. Above the doorway stands a flat, pierced tower containing three bells and marked by a wrought-iron cross. Inside, the long, narrow nave leads up to the finest altar in the San Antonio chain. Although not elaborate, it seems perfect for the space and reflects the honest feeling of a frontier church. On the left side of the

Misión San Juan Capistrano

The pierced tower of Misión San Juan Capistrano

San Juan Capistrano altar, with Ecce Homo on the left and Nuestra Señora de los Dolores on the right; note the two carved doors.

Detail of Nuestra Señora de los Dolores

nave stands a large figure of Christ in white—*Ecce Homo* —wearing a crown of thorns. On the opposite side is Nuestra Señora de los Dolores, a very old piece with a webbing of cracks in the delicately painted features. On either side of the reredos are wooden doors with carved panels depicting the Virgen de Guadalupe. The central figure on the reredos is San Juan Capis- trano, the fourteenth-century Italian theologian who had been a lawyer and governor of Perugia, Italy, before entering the Franciscan Order. In the true spirit of an inquisitor, he is dressed in armor and has pinned the head of a man firmly beneath his right foot.

The harsh contrasts embodied in the artwork of San Juan Capistrano make the Texas missions fascinating to explore. They provide a candid picture of the way religion and personal faith figured into the life of the early Southwest.

SAN FRANCISCO DE LA ESPADA

San Francisco de la Espada. The name is a strange contradiction: Saint Francis of the Sword. People have puzzled over the paradox for years. Like the church at San Juan Capistrano, Espada, as it is called, is a small, early chapel; it stands last on Mission Drive and survives the larger building that had been constructed to take its place.

The earliest mission bearing the name of San Francisco was the first mission in East Texas. It was established in 1690 on the Neches River as San Francisco de los Tejas. By 1693, problems with the Indians, disease, and increasing pressure from the French caused the closing of the mission. Father Damian

Espada seen through an opening in original mission ruins

Moorish doorway and wooden cross at Misión San Francisco de la Espada

121

Massanet described the final days in his diary: "Secretly the valuable ornaments were packed, the heavier articles, such as cannon, bells and other things of a similar nature were buried, and when everything was in readiness, on October 25, 1693, fire was applied to the Mission San Francisco de los Tejas, founded with so many sacrifices and with so much expense." In 1716, the mission was reestablished a few miles east of the original location. With the threat of a new invasion by the French, it was abandoned in 1719. In 1721, in yet another location, the mission became San Francisco de los Neches. It was closed in 1730 and moved briefly to the Colorado River. In 1731 it was established in its present site on the Río San Antonio.

Like its sister missions, Espada declined and suffered serious setbacks with the coming of secularization. It was a ruin until 1868, when it was restored through the ambitious efforts of Father François Bouchu. The bell tower, similar in style to the one at Capistrano, is a stone facade with openings for three bells. To the left of the Moorish doorway stands a large wooden cross. A woman of the parish explained that this cross had been carried about in the nineteenth century by members of the congregation who were praying for rain to relieve a severe summer drought. Their prayers brought an abundant rainfall, and the priest, the same Father Bouchu responsible for restoring the church, instructed the parishioners to position the cross near the doorway, as a reminder that prayers are answered. The cross has stood in that spot for over a hundred years.

Inside, the altar is plain, but graced with three bultos. On the right side of the nave stands Nuestra Señora de los Dolores, a figure frequently seen in the mission churches. Christ is on the left. San Francisco stands in the center, one foot on a globe, one hand raised, a gesture that some people feel indicates he once held a sword. If true, it would explain the word *espada* in the name of the church. However, that is a controversial view of Saint Francis, who was, perhaps, more likely holding his customary cross.

NUESTRA SEÑORA DEL CARMEN (ISLETA)

Nuestra Señora del Pilar del Paso del Río del Norte is the name the Spaniards first gave it in 1598, when Don Juan de Oñate stopped and took possession of New Mexico. And it was to El Paso that Don Antonio de Otermín, governor of New Mexico, fled at the time of the bloody 1680 Pueblo Revolt. At the friendly pueblo of Isleta, a few miles below present-day Albuquerque, he gathered the battered refugees from Santa Fe; their losses numbered over four hundred, including twenty-one Franciscan missionaries. Taking with them a number of Indians who had not joined in the rebellion, the party proceeded to El Paso. Governor Otermín, who had himself been wounded in the battle, established headquarters in San Lorenzo, a few miles south of El Paso, and set about creating a number of missions to provide for the Indian and Spanish refugees. This was nearly a decade before Alonso de León and Father Massanet founded Misión San Francisco on the Neches River—though it should be pointed out that in the seventeenth century El Paso was still considered part of the territory of New Mexico.

The topography of the El Paso area is quite different from that of East Texas or San Antonio. It is high and rugged, and the climate is fierce—hot and dry in the summer and cold in the winter. On the whole, the land here is less hospitable and less productive, except for the rich, arable soil confined to the area along the river, where the missions are located. U.S. Border Commissioner John Bartell wrote in his two-volume 1854 narrative: "About ten miles below [El Paso del Norte] is an island some twenty miles in length; it is one of the most fertile spots in the whole valley, and has been cultivated since the first settlement of the country." Other observers have commented on the abundant crops and especially the grapes that flourished in the valley and were made into excellent wine and brandy.

Of the mission churches built to serve the Indian and Spanish refugees, only two remain, Nuestra Señora del Carmen and Nuestra Señora de la Concepción del Socorro. A third structure of historical note is the chapel that was attached to the presidio at San Elizario.

Nuestra Señora del Carmen, which was originally called Corpus Christi de la Isleta and to which the refugees from San Agustín de la Isleta in New Mexico brought their patron saint, San Antonio de Padua, is the oldest of the mission churches in Texas. It still functions as a parish church for the Tigua Indians in Isleta.

The church has had its name changed three times. It was

Nuestra Señora del Carmen, in
Isleta, southeast of El Paso;
the church has also been called
San Antonio

Nuestra Señora del Carmen: small altar to the right of the main altar

called Corpus Christi de la Isleta by Governor Otermín. It was later called San Antonio de la Isleta—though this name may simply have been applied because of the figure of San Antonio that had been brought to the church from New Mexico. Today, although the church is known as Nuestra Señora del Carmen, the Indians, continuing the earlier tradition, celebrate on San Antonio Day.

In 1907 a serious fire destroyed the original church at Isleta. That building was very different, architecturally, from the present one. The church built since the fire is much squarer in appearance, and its tall silver dome dominates the pueblo.

Painted vigas supporting her-
ringbone-patterned latias in the
ceiling at Socorro

Distinctive facade of Nuestra
Señora de la Concepción del
Socorro

NUESTRA SEÑORA DE LA CONCEPCIÓN DEL SOCORRO

Nuestra Señora de la Concepción del Soccoro was originally located about twelve leagues from El Paso del Norte, a site somewhere near the small settlement of Fabens, Texas. While it was at that location, the Indians tried to kill their priest, Father Antonio Guerra. As a result, Governor Otermín relocated the mission settlement closer to Corpus Christi de la Isleta. In 1859 a flood crumbled the old Socorro church, and it was moved to where it now stands.

As with Nuestra Señora del Carmen, the name of Socorro has also changed. At first it was called Nuestra Señora del Socorro; then it was renamed La Purísima Concepción del Socorro. Locally, there are people who refer to the church as San Miguel because of the bulto of that saint that stands in the west transept of the church.

There is a popular story about how the statue of San Miguel came to be at the church. It was being hauled from Mexico to New Mexico in a cart pulled by oxen. When the cart reached the place where the church now stands it became stuck, and the oxen were unable to move it from that spot. Other teams of animals were gathered and tied to the wagon. Men tried to help. Nothing could move the wagon in which San Miguel rode. It was, obviously, a miracle, a sign that the saint wished to remain there and to serve the people at that place.

Nuestra Señora de la Concepción del Socorro: small altar in the east side of the transept, with San Miguel in the nicho

SAN ELIZARIO

Historians have concluded that La Toma, the place where Don Juan de Oñate first stopped on the Rio Grande in April 1598, was near the present village of San Elizario. It was there on April 30 that the new governor took possession of New Mexico; and a few days later, on May 4, he named El Paso del Norte.

The presidio eventually established at San Elizario has a history of peregrination similar to the missions at Isleta and Socorro. It was first built in 1774 in Valle de San Elizario, located near El Porvenir, approximately fifty-four miles south of Juárez. Six years later, it was moved to Hacienda de los Tiburcios, upriver to the spot where we now find San Elizario—locations substantiated on the Miera y Pecheco map of 1779. In a document from Lieutenant Governor Don Francisco Xavier Uranga, signed in Chihuahua on February 14, 1780, that move was officially announced:

San Elizario, facade with open-work bell tower

Rear view of the presidio chapel in San Elizario

Con esta fecha, se pasan los ordenes correspondientes para que el Teniente Coronel Don Francisco Martínez y Capitán de Eleceario Don Juan Antonio de Arce, se trasladen al Rancho de los Tiburcios, y en concurrencia de Vmd. reconoscan, y senalen el terreno donde convenga hacer la fábrica manual para ubicar la Companía de dicho San Eleceario.

(With this date, corresponding orders will be issued so that the Lieutenant Colonel Don Francisco Martínez and the Captain of San Eleceario Don Antonio de Arce will go to Rancho de los Tiburcios, for reconnaissance and to mark the land where it is convenient to build and locate the Company of said San Eleceario.)

The lieutenant governor went on to make it clear that forming adobes and gathering other supplies for the buildings was to begin immediately, before the onset of winter.

So, nearly a hundred years after the founding of the church at Isleta, the first San Elizario presidio chapel was built. *In Journal of a Soldier under Kearny and Doniphan 1846–1847*, George Rutledge Gibson wrote of the presidio and church that the "town has nothing about it different from other small places except a fort, which is capable of accommodating a large force and is really a strong place, the walls being both high and thick. The church is in the inside and is rather better furnished than similar buildings, but is on the gold and tinsel order."

The present building, begun in 1874, after the flooding Rio Grande destroyed the original church, faces the quiet plaza of San Elizario and contains little gold or tinsel. It is as paradoxical to learn that in the mid-nineteenth century San Elizario had become the largest town in West Texas, with a population of twelve hundred, six times that of El Paso, and was the county seat of El Paso County. Today, it is as quiet as the church, a small community of farmers that seems more Mexican than anything else.

CHURCHES
OF
CALIFORNIA

OAKLAND

15

SAN
FRANCISCO

SAN JOSE

280

101

1

SANTA CRUZ

WATSONVILLE

SAN JUAN
BAUTISTA

14

San Joaquin R.

FRESNO

MONTEREY

SALINAS

CARMEL

13

12

San Benito R.

G15

25

99

11

SAN LUCAS

JOLON

G18

198

10

SAN MIGUEL

PASO
ROBLES

46

Salinas R.

SAN LUIS
OBISPO

9

Tulare Lake

CALIFORNIA

14

101

166

58

8

7

33

15

LOMPOC

246

6

SANTA
INEZ

5

SANTA BARBARA

VENTURA

101

PASADENA

4

SAN GABRIEL

14

SAN
BERNARDINO

10

LOS ANGELES

5

91

3

1

SAN JUAN CAPISTRANO

OCEANSIDE

2

SAN CLEMENTE

76

1

8

SAN DIEGO

PACIFIC OCEAN

SIERRA NEVADA

NEVADA

N

395

OPENING ILLUSTRATION:
Nuestra Señora de la Soledad,
the thirteenth mission in the
great California chain

O n September 28, 1542, during an early voyage of exploration along the California coast, Captain Juan Rodríguez Cabrillo discovered a harbor, claimed it in the name of Spain, and called it San Miguel. Sixty years later, in November of 1602, Captain Sebastián Vizcaíno sailed into the same harbor. He recorded in his diary: "On the twelfth of the said month, which was the day of the glorious San Diego, the general, admiral, religious, captains, ensigns, and almost all the men went onshore. A hut was built and mass was said in celebration of the feast of Señor San Diego." In honor of the thirteenth-century Spanish saint, Captain Vizcaíno renamed the area San Diego.

California was the final frontier for Spanish expansion in the New World. In a certain sense, it had always been on the minds of the Spaniards; they had had glimpses of it and fantasized about its treasures for years. Periodic attempts were made at conquering the area—including expeditions of Cabrillo and Vizcaíno—but the crown was never quite prepared to make the kind of financial commitment necessary to create and maintain successful colonies so far north. Bitter over its heavy investments in New Mexico, Arizona, and Texas, which hadn't returned even a fraction of the wealth expended, the king was reluctant to try again.

It was only after the threat of an "invasion" by the Russians that Spain grew serious about moving into Alta California. The Russians—fur traders and explorers—had drifted down from the Bering Sea and set up a small working colony on the Farallon Islands, just off the coast of present-day San Francisco. For years, first the Jesuits and then the Franciscans had pressed for the colonization of Alta California, but their petitions had received little more than marginal interest from the Spanish crown —until the report of the Russian threat. Then Carlos III sent out the order that suddenly made colonization of California a priority.

Inspector General José de Gálvez organized the effort, designating Don Gaspár de Portolá, the newly appointed governor of Baja California, to head up the expedition and assume leadership of the new colonies. Also chosen from Baja California was Father Junípero Serra, whose job it would be to supervise the creation of the missions.

Like Father Kino in Pimeria Alta, Father Serra had a spe-

cial talent for missionary work, though he had begun it relatively late in life. He was born in Petra, Majorca, in 1713 and entered the Franciscan Order when he was sixteen. A devout, learned man, he spent the early years of his vocation as a seminary professor in Europe before becoming a missionary to Mexico.

Every step of the advance into California seemed to call for extraordinary sacrifice. Four groups left Mexico in this new, accelerated effort to establish colonies—two traveling by sea and two by land. Loaded with supplies and Spanish soldiers, the *San Carlos* steered out of La Paz in early January of 1769; a month later, the second ship, the *San Antonio*, with its cargo and soldiers, set sail for San Diego. Half of those who began the voyage died of scurvy; and those who made it ashore were sorely in need of rest and medical attention.

Hardships of a different nature beset the land expeditions.

Tile roof over the old monastery building, Misión Santa Barbara

Under the command of Captain Rivera, the first party departed from El Rosario on Good Friday, 1769. And the second, headed by Don Gaspár de Portolá, the group in which Father Serra traveled, started out in the middle of May. On the trail, the pace was hard. The burning sun was relentless; food and water were scarce. Men died and deserted. Those who finally reached San Diego were exhausted, and they were disheartened by what they saw. The Indians in the area were openly hostile; they took advantage of the weakened condition of the Spaniards, brazenly raiding their encampment and plundering their supplies.

Father Serra, daunted neither by the expedition's losses nor by the bleak prospects California seemed to offer, set about his work as missionary. He chose the location for a mission, and on July 16, 1769, raised the cross and said Mass, thereby founding San Diego de Alcalá, the first mission in Alta California.

SAN DIEGO DE ALCALÁ

Nestled back a few streets from the arterial roads that feed two busy Southern California freeways and seemingly oblivious to the furious bustle of a major city continuing to burgeon around it, San Diego de Alcalá possesses the air of a church from another, more tranquil time. The rough-hewn appearance of its white facade—with two oblique buttress walls reaching away from it and a towering campanario attached to one side—is a fitting monument to the first mission in the ambitious California chain. The simplicity of the facade and the rather whimsical design around the great front door echo something of the mission's history.

Five years after Father Serra sang Mass and erected the cross on Presidio Hill, where the original mission church was built, the site was moved northeast about six miles to the present location. The following year, 1775, the Indians raided the mis-

The reconstructed altar of San Diego de Alcalá, maintains the simplicity that was probably characteristic of the early mission.

Intricately detailed bulto of a seated Christ

sion, robbing the storerooms and the sacristy, and killing three men, including Father Luis Jayme, the first Franciscan martyr in Alta California. Father Jayme was mutilated beyond recognition; only his hands remained untouched, and it was by them that he was identified.

By the following October, a new church was built. It was enlarged in 1780 and badly damaged in the earthquake of 1803. The church constructed in its place was destroyed by yet another earthquake. After the rubble was cleared, a new structure was erected, this one with buttressed walls and other features designed to help it withstand the periodic tremors that plague California. It was dedicated on November 12, 1813.

Already the mission system was experiencing the political turmoil that resulted from New Spain's independence. The government of the Republic of Mexico, not the provider Spain had been, left the missions with little outside support.

Added to this was the confusion and instability brought on by secularization. Secularization had been built into the mission

Graceful, sweeping facade of San Diego de Alcalá; the oblique buttress walls are unique in all the missions.

Garden view of the sturdy San Diego campanario with its five massive bells, of which the largest, *Mater Dolorosa*, weighs over half a ton

plan from the beginning. After a period of ten years, during which the church fathers were to have civilized the Indians, the mission as a governing institution was to be dismantled and the Indians were to be given the mission land and allowed to live in a pueblo, under civil law and with the spiritual guidance of the priests who were to remain with the churches. In 1833 the Mexican government enacted a law that made that secularization policy mandatory. The secularization process was implemented and continued into the 1840s. In many ways its results were tragic. The Indians were unprepared for ownership and many of them were swindled out of their land by speculators and officials.

San Diego de Alcalá suffered with the other missions. It was appropriated in 1846 by the Mexican government and used as payment to Santiago Argüello for his services to the republic of Mexico. After the Mexican–American War, the mission was appropriated by the U.S. cavalry, and for the next fifteen years the army occupied its buildings. Finally, in response to an order issued by President Abraham Lincoln, a tract of twenty-two acres with the remaining buildings was returned to the Catholic Church.

The church and other buildings, after decades of misuse and neglect, were deteriorating. Then, near the end of the nineteenth century, Father Anthony Ubach began a campaign to restore the mission. His efforts were cut short by his death in 1907. A number of years later, the project was taken up again, and the mission, restored as closely as possible to the measurements of the original building, was rededicated in 1931.

No clear description of the interior of the church existed to give the restoration team the clues they needed to try to replicate the original building. However, going by what they found on the outside and by information learned from other, better-preserved missions, they kept the design simple and worked with the muted, earthy colors the Indians might have used in painting the walls. The interior, as we see it now, mirrors the quiet mood of the facade and captures a kind of timelessness that is possibly close to the feeling of the early nineteenth-century interior.

SAN CARLOS BORROMEO DE CARMELO
(CARMEL)

The mission church at San Carlos Borromeo de Carmelo illustrates the way most of the churches grew—incrementally. These sometimes all-too-temporary buildings were subject to the ravages of man, fate, and the raw life of the frontier. They were rebuilt, repaired, enlarged, altered, or improved each time they suffered a setback in the form of fire, earthquake, storm, or pillage.

The present church standing at Carmel, a name derived from the Carmelite priests who accompanied Captain Vizcaíno to the area in the seventeenth century, is the mission's seventh church and dates back to 1771. The first church, a simple log structure put up in Monterey the year before, shared a problem common to many mission churches on the frontier: it was situated too close to the Spanish garrison; the Indians, justifiably frightened of the Spanish soldiers, were reluctant to come into the mission. As a remedy for a situation that was compounding the difficulties of his work, Father Serra found a spot some five miles from Monterey and relocated the mission. Not only had he solved the problem of the soldiers, there were also better growing conditions at the new location, and he was closer to the Indian villages.

Father Serra loved Carmelo, the people and the countryside, and he once described it as "the garden of God." As proof of his affection, he made it his headquarters and ran the entire mission chain from there.

San Carlos Borromeo: the quadrangle and church with a star-shaped window

The stone church, San Carlos Borromeo de Carmelo, completed in 1797, after the death of Father Serra, who had long planned to have it built

Serra had good reason to believe the missionaries would be successful in converting the Indians he found near Monterey Bay. When the party scouting for the mission reached Monterey, they began to hunt for the marker Portolá had left on his earlier trip. When they located it, the whole party stopped in astonished silence. The four-foot cross had obviously become a shrine for the Indians. The ground around it was covered with carefully placed arrows that pointed inward to the cross. Hanging from the cross was a string of small fresh fish and, beneath them, was an arrangement of mussels. At various intervals, eagle feathers quilled out of the dirt to form what seemed to be a meaningful pattern. Later, the Indians confessed that, at night, this cross, which they had watched since Portolá had planted it, would take on an eerie luminosity that seemed to reach into the heavens.

Father Serra did not live to see the stone church in which he is buried. Before his death he had made arrangements for the stone to be quarried from the nearby mountains, and there is speculation that he might even have drawn out a design for the church, which was begun the year before his death.

Juan Ruiz, a master stonemason, was brought in to build the chapel at Monterey as well as the church at Carmel. In 1793, the cornerstones were laid at Carmel. Ruiz, assisted mainly by Indians, continued to work on the church for four years; it was dedicated in 1797.

The stone church at San Carlos Borromeo is a unique mixture of architectural elements. There are two unmatched bell towers in front and the unusual carved Moorish window set into the stones above the front doors. One has the feeling that Ruiz's intention for the window was one thing and the window that was the result is another. One possible explanation for this is that Juan Ruiz's helpers were untrained Indians with only limited experience. The window's basic motif, its Moorish shape, is carried into the interior where—at least in the arched entrance to the mortuary chapel—it is repeated.

During the decline of the mission system, San Carlos held up no better than its sister churches. Robert Louis Stevenson described it in its worst state: "a ruined mission on a hill." He continued, "From the mission church the eye embraces a great field of ocean, and the ear is filled with a continuous sound of distant breakers on the shore. The roof has fallen; the ground-squirrel scampers on the grass; the holy bell of St. Charles is long dismounted; yet one day in every year the church awakes from silence, and the Indians return to worship in the church of their converted fathers."

A serene moment in one of the mission gardens

The curiously mismatched bell towers at San Carlos—one of Moorish design, the other more conventionally Spanish

SAN ANTONIO DE PADUA

Inadvertently, San Antonio de Padua, the third mission founded by Father Serra, retains to this day a strange and unsettling tie to the old missions: it is still surrounded by soldiers. On the day I drove into the area—once known as Los Robles, or the Oaks—I was forced to wait while a convoy of troop carriers passed through the gates of the military preserve, bearing teenage soldiers in camouflage jungle fatigues, their faces smudged with black and their helmets bristling with fresh-picked foliage. A chopper, outfitted for combat, hovered for a moment, then, dropping its nose slightly, skimmed away through the shimmering heat, heading south and disappearing over a ridge. The soldier on gate duty directed me to the mission and then stepped back sharply.

The jarring experience of seeing combat-ready soldiers and a helicopter gunship reminded me of a story I had read connected with the early days of the mission. An Indian woman named Agüeda, who was over a hundred years old, came to the priests at San Antonio de Padua and asked to be baptized. When they questioned her intentions she told them that a number of

San Antonio de Padua, the main reredos: All the bultos are original—San Antonio holds a child, symbolic of his devotion to the Christ child.

Original bulto of San Antonio

years before, men dressed in garb similar to their simple priest's robes had come out of the sky in strange ships and offered her people the message of Christianity. They had been gone for a long time, but she had made up her mind to accept.

San Antonio de Padua, founded July 14, 1771, now stands about a mile and a half from the first site. This church, the third of that name, was begun in 1810. The unique campanario, with its arches and openings for three bells, was added some time after the building was completed; behind it, a barrel vault leads to the entrance of the church. After secularization, both church and mission were virtually abandoned for almost fifty years. An enthusiastic restoration effort instituted by the California Historic Landmarks League got under way in 1903 but was hampered by various disasters. Heavy rains melted away the adobe, and then the whole structure was brought down by the 1906 earthquake. The work of rebuilding resumed, and the church was completed in 1907.

The restored church, with its beamed ceiling, is decorated with many of the original bultos. The archway leading into the sanctuary has been painted pale blue and patterned with stars. At the top of the walls and from a point just above the pews down to the floor are painted designs in soft colors meant to duplicate the feeling of the originals. Behind the altar, the reredos, dominated by San Antonio, who holds a child, exemplary of his devotion to the Christ child, is simple in design but beautifully painted.

The long facade of San Antonio de Padua, behind which is the enclosed quadrangle, shows the vast and complex nature of the original mission.

Facade, showing the campanario built in front of the church and roofed over to create a barrel vault

SAN GABRIEL ARCÁNGEL

The mission San Gabriel Arcángel, named after the angel of the Annunciation who appeared to Mary in Nazareth to inform her of her destiny, was founded not far from a river called Río de los Temblores, River of the Earthquakes, by Father Ángel Fernández de la Somera and Father Pedro Benito Cambón, under the direction of Father Junípero Serra. The name of the river was all too apt. When I made my first trip into the area to photograph the mission church, an earthquake had shaken the region, and I arrived to find the church closed due to dangerous structural damage. It was some months before the repairs were completed and I could return to shoot any photographs.

As in almost all of the missions, the resident priests whose job it was to construct the church were largely men without professional direction. They added to the buildings whatever they thought was appropriate in the way of design. Acting in this fashion, at least two priests shaped the appearance of the church at

The lines of the campanario were inspired by Father José Maria Zalvedia. The tall windows and the design of the buttresses reflect Moorish influences in Spanish architecture.

The unusual capped buttresses of San Gabriel have been credited to Father Antonio Cruzado.

157

San Gabriel. Certain aspects of the exterior—particularly the capped buttresses and the high, elongated windows, reminiscent of the Moorish influences in Spanish architecture—are credited to Father Antonio Cruzado, who oversaw the construction of a great portion of the original church. Father Cruzado was a native of Alcarazegos, a town in Andalusia near Córdova, a city that had been transformed by the Moors between the eighth and the eleventh centuries. Another priest, Father José María Zalvedia, was responsible for the campanario affixed to the side wall of the structure; he had it built to replace the bell tower that had stood at the north front corner of the church until it was toppled by an earthquake.

In spite of the numerous earthquakes and the attrition of time, there is preserved in the interior of the church the original altar, brought from Mexico City in the final decade of the eighteenth century, as well as six polychromed Spanish bultos of the same period. At least a hundred years older are the paintings of the Apostles and a painting of Nuestra Señora de los Dolores which stands to the left of the altar. It is said to have saved the lives of the members of the founding party. When they reached the site Father Serra had designated for the mission, they were met by a large number of armed Indians. One of the priests, either Father Somera or Father Cambón, unrolled the painting and held it up before the Indians. Immediately, they put down their weapons and many of them paid homage to Nuestra Señora by removing their beads and leaving them as offerings.

The original campanario was built onto the front of the church; after it toppled, Father Zalvedia had its replacement built at the back of the church.

The rather plain facade of San Gabriel Arcángel

SAN LUIS OBISPO DE TOLOSA

Unlike so many of her sister missions, San Luis Obispo de Tolosa was not moved from the site Father Serra originally chose. Father Serra had the idea of establishing a mission that would tie the two southern missions, San Diego de Alcalá and San Gabriel Arcángel, with the two northern missions, San Carlos Borromeo de Carmelo and San Antonio de Padua, but the time to build it had never been quite right. Then, in 1772, with the entire mission chain suffering from a lack of supplies, soldiers were dispatched to El Valle de los Osos, a region Portolá had found to be heavily populated by bears in 1769, and ordered to bring back meat. Over a busy period of three months, the soldiers dried nine thousand pounds of bear jerky for mission use and traded more bear to the Indians for a quantity of edible seeds—all of which was encouraging to Father Serra.

Eventually, the ships carrying provisions for the missions arrived in San Diego, and Serra decided to travel down and per-

Interior of San Luis Obispo de Tolosa, including the nave leading up to the main altar with its painted reredos holding a bulto of San Luis

This painting, set back in a small decorated alcove, is of Our Lady of Refuge.

Originally completed in 1772, San Luis Obispo de Tolosa remained on its original spot. Like many missions here and in other states, it was remodeled and changed many times before it was finally restored to the Spanish style in the 1930s.

suade the captains to bring their cargo on to Monterey. Acting on stories brought back by the soldiers and his own conviction that he should now establish the fifth mission in spite of the economics against it, Father Serra scheduled a stop in El Valle de los Osos, the Valley of the Bears. He brought with him Father José Cavaller, a new priest from Spain, and the few supplies they could spare from San Carlos Borromeo de Carmelo. Father Serra selected the site, a Mass was said, and the mission was dedicated in the name of San Luis, a thirteenth-century bishop of Toulouse, France, who had once refused a kingdom offered to him by his father, saying: "Jesus Christ is my kingdom. If I possess him alone, I shall have all things; if I have him not, I lose all."

The adobe church at San Luis Obispo, built in 1793, has been the object of numerous instances of accident, violence, and whim. It burned at least twice in the eighteenth century. It was rebuilt and remodeled. Once, the original structure was encased in wooden clapboard siding, and the bells were moved from the old facade to a tower comically reminiscent of nineteenth-century New England churches. Finally, in the mid-1930s, the wood was stripped away and, along with the rest of the mission, the church was restored to the old Spanish style and enlarged to accommodate a growing parish. Today, betraying no clues to its mercurial past, the facade of the church seems solid, almost imposing. The inside is quiet and unpretentious. The altar is dominated by San Luis, but the painting of Nuestra Señora del Refugio, on the right-hand side of the nave and lighted by a single fixture attached to the frame, is easily the most arresting piece of art in the chapel.

SAN FRANCISCO DE ASÍS
(MISIÓN DOLORES)

There is a famous story predating the founding of San Francisco de Asís, the great mission in San Francisco. It seems Father Serra remarked that no mission had yet been named for St. Francis, the founder of the Franciscan Order. Tauntingly, Visitor General José de Gálvez, who was working with him on plans for the first three missions, replied: *"Si San Francisco quiere misión, que haga se halla su puerto y se le pondrá."* ("If St. Francis wants a mission, let him show us his port and one will be put there for him.")

In due time, the San Francisco Bay was discovered. José de Ortega, a sergeant, found it while scouting ahead of Gaspar de Portolá's 1769 expedition to locate Monterey Bay. The promised mission followed, constructed on a site near Arroyo de Nuestra Señora de los Dolores. Work on the church began April 25, 1782,

The main reredos in Misión Dolores is as richly gilded as any at its sister mission, San Carlos Borromeo de Carmelo.

More sophisticated than many other mission interiors, San Francisco de Asís, often called Misión Dolores, boasts numerous nineteenth-century Mexican reredoses and bultos.

was completed nearly three years later, and the building was dedicated on April 3, 1791. But despite the good intentions of Father Serra and others, the name San Francisco de Asís has never stuck. The mission has always been known—unofficially—as Dolores.

Relatively few alterations have been made to the church. Dolores survived the devastations of the 1906 earthquake and subsequent fire, needing only cosmetic repairs, some shoring up, and a general strengthening that was carried out as much for protection against future quakes as to repair existing damage. In fact, the church has stood by for over a century while the mission building directly to the north has been altered, enlarged, demolished, and completely replaced. Once a convento and storehouse, it has also served as a seminary, until the entire structure was taken down and a parish church was built in its place; the parish church was damaged by the 1906 earthquake, replaced, and finally remodeled into the basílica that stands on the spot today.

On the inside, Dolores exhibits the same rich texture as San Carlos Borromeo. The gold reredos as well as the bultos in the altar niches, brought to San Francisco from Mexico in the early nineteenth century, are more sophisticated than much of the art found in other mission churches. Except for regilding, they have been left unchanged since their installation. The ceiling has been repainted in recent years, but it still bears the motifs designed and painted by the Indians for whom the mission was built.

Misión San Francisco de Asís has remained virtually unchanged since its completion in 1791.

Sunlight strikes a figure in the campo santo at the side of San Francisco de Asís.

SAN JUAN CAPISTRANO

Fountain inside the quadrangle
at San Juan Capistrano

Ruined walls of the great San
Juan Capistrano church, which
fell in December of 1812

Songs, poems, books, and films have celebrated the swallows, the bells, the wealth, and the plight of the mission San Juan Capistrano. But even more remarkable are its less familiar history as a working mission and the history of its two great churches.

The seventh mission in the California chain, San Juan Capistrano was founded twice. On October 30, 1775, Father Fermín Francisco Lasuén, accompanied by Father Amurrio from mission San Gabriel, brought the bells and other items they would need and founded it the first time. Father Francisco Palóu described the event: "On arriving at the site, an enramada or arbor was hastily erected, near which a large cross was constructed, raised, blessed, and venerated by all. On an altar prepared in the arbor, Fr. Lasuén offered up the first holy Mass. This happened on . . . the last day of the octave after the feast of San Juan Capistrano, the patron of the mission."

OPPOSITE AND THIS PAGE:
Interior of "Father Serra's
church." The massive gilt reredos, from Barcelona, was
added some time in the 1920s.

The mission was barely blessed and the work of building begun when word came from the south that there had been a violent Indian uprising at San Diego de Alcalá. Stunned by the news and concerned for the lives of their fellow priests, the two missionaries hastily buried the bells and returned.

A year later, Father Serra, Father Pablo Mugartegui and Father Amurrio made their way back to the site, where the cross still stood. They dug up the bells and enacted a new founding ceremony on November 1, 1776, again naming the mission after the remarkable fourteenth-century Italian theologian San Juan de Capistrano.

Father Serra had a special place in his heart for San Juan Capistrano and its first church, where he occasionally sang Mass and presided at confirmations. Father Serra's Church—as it is called today—claims to be both the oldest building in California and the only surviving church in that state where Serra himself had said Mass.

At the close of the century, a second, much larger church was built at San Juan Capistrano. This great building, planned by Father Gregorio and constructed of stone, was in the form of a Roman cross, its nave measuring 18 by 180 feet and transept arms extending to 40 feet. Under the guidance of a master mason, using stone quarried six miles away and brought to the mission by the Indians, it grew into a magnificent structure, the most glorious of all the mission churches. Worked into its arched roof were seven domes. Its tall, two-tiered bell tower, housing four great bells, could once be seen from as far away as ten miles. After nine years of construction, the dedication took place on September 8, 1806.

The church was destined to last barely six years before it was demolished by an earthquake in December of 1812.

The great church was never rebuilt; its ruins are home to the thousands of swallows that flock to it every March 19, St. Joseph's Day. Today, Father Serra's Church, which outlived the huge edifice in whose shadow it once stood, continues to serve. In the 1920s the massive gilt reredos was added. This handsome piece, made in the seventeenth century and brought over from Barcelona, was originally intended for use in Los Angeles; it remained in storage for almost two decades before it was brought to San Juan Capistrano. Its sumptuousness is at first overwhelming; but, in an odd way, it fits with the crude Indian wall paintings, the bultos, and the stations of the cross that have survived since the early days of the mission.

SAN BUENAVENTURA

Under La Loma de la Cruz, the Hill of the Cross, where the soaring cross, visible from both land and sea, was raised in preparation for the dedication of the mission on Easter Sunday of 1782, stands the San Buenaventura church. San Buenaventura was the ninth California mission and the last one founded by Father Junípero Serra, who died two years later, on August 28, 1784. The father president, accompanied by a comparatively large party, including Governor Neve and a troop of his soldiers, performed Mass and consecrated the mission to God in the name of San Buenaventura, the great thirteenth-century Italian scholar and theologian.

San Buenaventura was the last church founded by Junípero Serra.

One of the church's tiled fountains

The mission was built to serve the Chumash Indians, a people whose culture was advanced beyond many of the California tribes. Good-natured, artistic, and willing to work, the Chumash were excellent basketmakers, weaving the reeds into fine tight vessels capable of holding water.

The facade of the present mission church, which was rebuilt after the 1812 earthquake, seems to have undergone few significant alterations. There remains the same curious triangular-shaped trim above the front door and an awkward mass to the base of the bell tower, which appears in many old drawings and photographs.

However, the interior of the church suffered badly at the hands of one priest who, with all the best intentions, set about to modernize the building and bring it up to date. It is a familiar and painful story, repeated in every area of the frontier. Father Rubio's "improvements" consisted of tearing out and discarding the old wooden reredos, covering the beamed ceiling with tongue-in-groove sheeting, reshaping the windows, adding a wooden floor above the old paving stones, and covering over the Indian wall paintings. One feature he fortunately overlooked was the west door, with its spectacular Moorish cut and the design surrounding it. In 1957, a restoration returned the church interior to something close to the appearance it had had before Father Rubio's unfortunate tenure.

San Buenaventura's sturdy bell tower and unusual graphic facade—a triangular form above the arched doorway—are seen from across a tiled public fountain.

SANTA BARBARA

It is a curious juxtaposition to view the Roman facade of the Santa Barbara mission church across the waters of the lavandería fed by the Moorish fountain—built in 1808—which stands in front of the monastery. Inspiration for the classic facade was drawn from a Spanish edition of a first-century B.C. work on architecture by Vitruvius. That such a model was chosen for this church is an instructive example of the capricious nature of mission design. The entrance to the church, decorated on top with statues of Faith, Hope, and Charity, somehow stretches between and incorporates the two rather ponderous mission-style bell

The garden at Santa Barbara

Built in 1808 as the tenth California mission, Santa Barbara blends Roman design with more familiar Spanish and Moorish architectural ideas in probably the most striking facade of the entire chain.

towers. The apparently incongruous aesthetics work in much the same way as the Moorish ideas work with the early architecture of Spain; the effect is at first jarring but not unpleasant.

Santa Barbara was named and blessed in December 1786, and the mission grew and flourished. Its first church was replaced by a second, larger adobe church; that, in turn, was replaced by an even larger church, which perished in the 1812 earthquake. The present church, completed in 1820, suffered serious damage from another quake in 1925, but it was rebuilt and thoroughly reinforced against future tremors.

The inside of the church at Santa Barbara is richly textured

Santa Barbara, reflected in the
waters of the mission fountain

with wall painting. There are designs painted at the base of the walls, as a border near the ceiling, and around doorways; some are geometric, others are floral. Niches and windows are patterned to imitate marble or wood. The effect is to give the church and the small chapel to the left of the main altar a human scale and warmth and thus tie it to the mission tradition.

At the top of the magnificent main altar is a crucifix. Large, beautifully crafted figures of Santa Barbara in the center, with La Purísima Concepción and San José on either side, stand on the middle row. Two smaller figures, Santo Domingo and San Francisco, are below them, at opposite sides of the reredos.

Santa Barbara escaped the fate of secularization and the subsequent decay that crippled many other missions. The Franciscan Fathers never gave up their claim to the property. The bishop moved his residence from San Diego to Santa Barbara in 1842, and shortly thereafter the mission was made a college where Franciscan novitiates came to study. It has continued to grow and serve in the same capacity since that time.

Detail of Roman ornamentation

OVERLEAF, LEFT:
The simple altar in the small chapel to the left of the nave

OVERLEAF, RIGHT:
Santa Barbara dominates the reredos in the richly painted interior of the church.

LA PURÍSIMA
CONCEPCIÓN DE MARÍA SANTÍSIMA

Father Fermín Francisco Lasuén, continuing the work of Father Serra, blessed the first site of the eleventh mission, Misión La Purísima Concepción de María Santísima (Mission of the Immaculate Conception of the Most Holy Mary), on December 8, 1787. It was located south of the Santa Inez River near the center of present-day Lompoc.

La Purísima Concepción rapidly developed into a successful community, partly because of the excellent guidance of Father Mariano Payéras. Then, in 1812, the year when most of the missions in the California chain sustained earthquake damage, La Purísima Concepción was hit especially hard. The first tremors, coming on December 8, exactly twenty-five years after the founding ceremony, did little damage; however, on December 21, a series of brutal quakes struck. They were followed by rain, a deluge that reduced much of the broken adobe construction to mud.

Almost immediately Father Payéras gathered up his community and moved it to La Cañada de los Berros, the Valley of the Watercress, which lay some five miles away. A new, though temporary, church was erected of poles faced with adobe mud.

The church viewed from a portal of the monastery building

OPPOSITE:
The rather plain facade of the church at La Purísima Concepción. The campanario at the far end leads into the wall of the campo santo.

Intricately detailed confessional in the monastery chapel at La Purísima Concepción

LEFT AND OVERLEAF:
The campo santo gate and church at Misión La Purísima Concepción, as restored by C.C.C. workers in a project completed in 1941

185

When this structure finally collapsed in 1818, another was built. Three years later, the campo santo, or cemetery, was walled in, and a bell tower was added to the end of the church. Also in use at La Purísima was a small chapel built at one end of the monastery.

With the secularization decree of Governor José Figueroa in 1834, life at La Purísima changed drastically. The resident priests abandoned the mission and moved twenty-five miles to Santa Inez, a newer mission that had been established on El Camino Real between La Purísima and Santa Barbara. After that, only on rare occasions were services ever held in the church or the small monastery chapel.

In 1934 members of the Civilian Conservation Corps (CCC) began a careful restoration of La Purísima Concepción; the crew included architects, archaeologists, historians, and engineers. Working together until 1941, they were able to refurbish the church and other buildings. Today, the mission complex, including both the church and the small chapel, is protected as a state park and provides a fascinating glimpse of how a mission must have functioned.

Going out from the visitor center, the pathway leads to the campo santo behind a high wall capped with the same terracotta tiles that cover the roofs of the buildings. To the right is the church, a long room with neither pews nor chairs; typical of early mission churches, where Indians simply knelt on the floor for services. Located behind the church are the tallow vats. The next building houses the shops and quarters of the majordomo and others—blacksmith, potter, carpenter, saddlemaker, weaver, and so on. At the west end of the long building where the priests had their quarters is a small monastery church. Behind it is the pottery and the kitchen. Standing apart from the other buildings are the Indians' dormitories and the infirmaries. La Purísima Concepción, like all the missions, functioned as a complete unit. It was complex, workable, and self-sustaining. With the church at its heart and the priests as spiritual and temporal leaders, it became a powerful force in the lives of the Indians and in all life on the frontier.

SAN JUAN BAUTISTA

The "river of life" design on exterior door leading into the courtyard at San Juan Bautista

In San Juan Bautista, I waited while a huge tank of a car, billowing oil smoke and lurching along on not more than four of its eight cylinders, chugged into the parking lot west of the mission. A beautiful woman in a pastel dress climbed out of the battered car. She paused a second then reached back inside for a square pillow covered in pink silk. In front of the mission church she met a small group that included a teenage bride in a white gown and a groom in a tieless white shirt, pressed trousers, and cowboy boots whose pointed toes were buffed to a glassy shine. The entire wedding party numbered no' more than fifteen, half of whom seemed to be younger brothers and sisters of the bride. Inside, they made their way to the front of the church and huddled on the first two benches, while the priest recited the vows in Spanish—as they had been repeated for almost two hundred years.

San Juan Bautista, the fifteenth mission, has the distinction of being located right at the edge of the disastrous San Andreas fault. Perhaps because of this, it has never been damaged as badly during a quake as some missions farther from the fault.

The present church, an enlarged replacement for the first church at San Juan Bautista, was begun in 1803 and completed and dedicated fifteen years later. The building was shaped by unusual circumstances. Father Felipe del Arroyo de la Cuesta came to the mission while the building was under construction. He convinced the other fathers to rethink their plans and expand the building to three aisles instead of one, thus giving them room for their growing congregation. The new plan went ahead, with wide arched supports to carry the extra roof and create the additional aisles. However, at some time during the long period of construction the fathers questioned the wisdom of their earlier decision, filled in the side arches to better support the roof, and ended up with the single-aisle nave they originally had in mind.

The fathers made another unusual decision concerning the look of San Juan Bautista. A Mexican painter had been hired to decorate the reredos, but he was asking to be paid the equivalent of seventy-five cents a day for his work, a price the priests thought too high. Thomas Doaks, a sailor from Boston who had jumped ship in Monterey, offered to do the job for only his room and board. His offer was accepted, and he went to work. His paintings are workmanlike, with a naive charm; indeed, they are remarkable for their color, which has held up brilliantly for over 170 years.

Small altar at the rear of the south nave. The paintings in the church were done by Thomas Doaks, an itinerant sailor who was hired by the padres after they decided the fee asked by the Mexican painter originally contracted to do the work was too high.

Altar in one of the secondary naves at San Juan Bautista

In the reredos, San Juan Bautista, the patron saint, occupies the center niche. Directly above him is San Pascual. San Antonio is in the upper left niche, San Francisco beneath him; San Isidoro stands in the upper right niche and Santo Domingo is in the lower right.

One of the great priests to serve at San Juan Bautista was Father Estévan Tápis, who put together a remarkable Indian boys choir and established here a tradition of music education that continued for years. His method of teaching was to color-code his large parchment scores so each of the voices followed different colored notes. After the death of Father Tápis, the choir continued as a strong feature of the mission. One group of its members was so concerned that they might weaken and take to drinking on Saturday night that they asked the priest to lock them in the jail until Sunday morning—so they would be able to sing.

SAN MIGUEL ARCÁNGEL

If Doaks's work in San Juan Bautista was simple though expressive, the painting seen in the interior of the San Miguel church in the sixteenth-century California mission exhibits artistry of the highest order.

The painter was Catalonia-born, a friend of the resident priest, Father Juan Martín. Assisted by a number of Indian apprentices, this artist, Estévan Munras, created a world unto itself on the walls inside the adobe church. His palette is bright, his imagination vivid. To the simple adobe room he brought imagination and charm; he gave it depth by painting in columns, doorways, and balconies. His reredos creates a spectacular framing

The gate at San Miguel Arcángel, a mission known for its unique cactus gardens

This curious stonework campanario at San Miguel Arcángel was constructed in the 1950s.

The fountain at San Miguel Arcángel, patterned after the fountain at Santa Barbara, was added during a restoration.

The pulpit, with its unusual sounding board, beneath which hangs a white dove, symbol of the Holy Ghost

for the figure of San Miguel. Above the saint is the all-seeing eye of God, with blue sky, clouds, and the dazzling rays of a beneficent sun. The pulpit against the north wall is curious, with its unusual shape and its sounding board—from which hangs a white dove, symbolizing the Holy Spirit.

Founded on July 25, 1797, the same summer as the fourteenth mission, San José de Guadalupe (located near the present city of San Jose), and San Juan Bautista, San Miguel Arcángel lost its first church to fire; construction of a new, larger church was delayed until 1816. In the meantime, Father Martín, anticipating his new church, set the mission Indians to work forming, drying, and stockpiling adobe bricks. Once the actual building was under way, this store of materials greatly reduced the building time, and the church was completed in 1818. Estévan Munras's paintings were added in 1820.

It is something of a miracle that San Miguel has survived in such good condition. After secularization, other parts of the mission were sold and used for various purposes. At one time, they housed a tavern as well as a dealership for sewing machines. The William Reed family lived in one wing for years—indeed, until 1849, when they and their servants were murdered by a group of ne'er-do-wells.

In 1859 the mission was returned to the Church, but it was thirty-six years before San Miguel was again put into use. In 1928 it was given to the Franciscans for a parish church and monastery.

SAN LUIS REY DE FRANCIA

The mission San Luis Rey de Francia has served as the backdrop for a number of movies couched in California history, including the popular Zorro films. The reasons for this are obvious. San Luis Rey epitomizes the frontier mission. It is sweeping and romantic. The church, with its single bell tower, dominates the entire facade of the remaining mission complex. Stark white against the blue California sky, its elegant, flowing outline is unmatched by that of any other mission.

San Luis Rey, the eighteenth mission, established June 13, 1789, by Father Fermín Francisco Lasuén, was named in honor

OPPOSITE:
San Luis Rey de Francia, view toward the rear

FAR LEFT AND ABOVE:
Terra-cotta figures in nichos on either side of the doorway to the church

LEFT:
Detail of facade of San Luis Rey de Francia

Designed by Father Peyri, the facade of San Luis Rey is perhaps the most beautiful of the California missions.

The main altar and reredos at San Luis Rey. The reredos is dominated by the crucifix, and above that the San Luis Rey de Francia.

of Louis IX, the French king canonized for his crusades into the Holy Land and Egypt during the thirteenth century. Construction of the large church, with its 138-foot nave, was begun in 1811. Four years later, the building was complete and ready to be dedicated.

It was constructed of odd-size adobe blocks that measured eight inches square by twenty-four inches long. After the collapse of the great church at San Juan Capistrano, San Luis Rey remained the only mission church in the California chain built in the shape of a huge cross. Also unique is the double-domed ceiling constructed of wood and opening to an octagonal lantern in the top.

Through an entryway on the right-hand side of the nave is a small mortuary chapel. Under a domed ceiling, the octagonal room—the shape carried over from the domes over the transept —features a handsome altar set deep in a large niche. Richly detailed with marbleized columns, painted wall decoration, and old oil paintings, this chapel is the most striking in the entire California chain.

The priest responsible for much of the construction and the successful operation of the mission properties was Father Antonio Peyri. Fresh from Spain and a brief period of instruction in Mexico, Father Peyri came to San Luis Rey in its earliest days and continued to shape the mission and its destiny for over thirty years. Finally, as difficulties with the Mexican authorities—who had taken over from the Spanish—grew more and more distasteful, he chose to leave the mission.

It must have been a painful decision, for Father Peyri had invested his whole life in San Luis Rey. He rode away from the mission late one night, traveling by horseback to San Diego where he boarded a ship bound for Mexico the next day. When Indians at the mission discovered that he had gone, they raced after him, a large group of them reaching the port just as the ship carrying their beloved Father Peyri was sailing out of the harbor.

The final farewell between priest and congregation was said at a distance, with the waving of hands and the solemnly drawn sign of the cross.

Side altar in the nave

SANTA INÉS

Gradually, the gaps in El Camino Real were filled. Santa Inés, the nineteenth mission, was established between Santa Barbara and La Purísima Concepción on the east side of the Coast Range in the Santa Ynez valley, where Father Lasuén felt that a rich harvest of souls awaited the missionaries. On September 17, 1804, the cross was set and the mission dedicated by Father Estévan Tápis.

Like so many mission churches in California, the first church at Santa Inés, completed in the year following its dedication, fell with the 1812 earthquake. The church that now stands was completed in 1817. To the right of the nave stands the pierced campanario; although it was replaced twice, it still contains the original bells. Attached to the left side of the church is a section of the mission that served as quarters for the priests. A row of beautiful arches runs along the front of it. When the mission was intact, there were a total of twenty-four arches.

The colonnade at Santa Inés once stretched to twenty-two arches; today there are only half that number.

Seen from the rear is the campanario, which extends out from the front wall of the church

Elements of solid Spanish architecture are evident in the white plaster and terra-cotta tiles of Santa Inés.

Interior of the vividly repainted chapel at Misión Santa Inés

The designs inside the church have been vividly repainted. The reredos is dominated by the figure of Santa Inés, the thirteen-year-old Roman girl who was martyred in the fourth century. Standing against a green shell suited to the motif of the reredos, she holds a lamb. As at San Miguel and Santa Barbara, along the nave there are trompe l'oeil paintings in which elaborate architectural details have been applied to the otherwise plain plastered walls to lend them interest.

There is an unusual story concerning the church at Mission Santa Inés. With the threat of secularization, the life of the missions was in serious jeopardy. To make things worse, from 1821 on, there was little or no financial support for the presidios and their soldiers. They began taking their food and other supplies from the missions, making payment in the form of drafts, which were never honored—and probably never intended to be. This created a hardship for the missions, as the major burden of these

Detail from reredos at Santa Inés. Santa Inés, holding a lamb and palm, was a thirteen-year-old Roman girl martyred in the fourth century.

new demands fell on the mission Indians. Resentment grew. Tension increased. Finally, on Sunday, February 21, 1824, a guard at Santa Inés beat an Indian from La Purísima. The Indians rebelled and took up arms against the soldiers. In the midst of the battle, fire broke out and spread to the roof of the church. Both the Indians and the soldiers stopped fighting and combined their efforts to extinguish the blaze. When that danger was over, they resumed the battle.

Secularization, forced on the missions in 1834, brought hard times to Santa Inés. Within two years, part of it was being rented to José Covarrubias. The priests stayed in the section of the mission attached to the church. In 1843, the year the fathers again became proprietors of Santa Inés, a seminary, the College of Our Lady of Refuge, was started in the mission compound. After three years, it was moved and arrangements were made to sell the land to José Covarrubias and a partner. That transaction was never completed. The United States, which had tried on a number of occasions to purchase California, took advantage of the war with Mexico and seized the territory.

During the next half century little was done to restore or even to keep the church repaired. One Sunday, while the priest was in the pulpit delivering his sermon, the floor gave way under him. It wasn't until the first decades of the twentieth century that Santa Inés, through the efforts of Father Alexander Buckler and Mamie Goulet, was finally restored.

San Juan Bautista, along with all the churches in the California chain and the great early churches of Texas, Arizona, and New Mexico, was the result of Spain's twofold purpose of increasing the wealth and holdings of the Spanish crown and spreading Christianity throughout the New World. The Spanish priests, Jesuits and Franciscans, were well-intentioned, if sometimes simply wrong, and their efforts at building churches often reached heroic proportions. Today, the churches themselves serve a dual function. Most of them operate as parish churches, for congregations that include descendants of the conquistadors, colonists, and Indians who were members of the original missions and colonizing communities. Although many churches were sold and later returned to the Catholic Church after having been remodeled or completely rebuilt, they are all national treasures, monuments that retain the spirit of the frontier and remind us of a chapter in our history that is barely beginning to receive the recognition it deserves.

Bibliography

Adams, Eleanor B., and Fray Angelico Chavez, eds. *The Missions of New Mexico, 1776*. Albuquerque: The University of New Mexico Press, 1956.

Baer, Kurt. *Architecture of the California Missions*. Berkeley: University of California Press, 1958.

Bancroft, Hubert Howe. *History of Arizona and New Mexico, 1530–1888*. Albuquerque: Horn and Wallace, 1962.

————. *Texas in the Middle Eighteenth Century*. Berkeley: University of California Press, 1955.

Bandelier, Adolf F. *The Southwestern Journals of Adolf F. Bandelier, 1880–1882*. Albuquerque: University of New Mexico Press, 1966.

Bannon, John Francis, ed. *Bolton and the Spanish Borderlands*. Norman: University of Oklahoma Press, 1964.

Barnes, Thomas C., Thomas H. Naylor, and Charles W. Polzer. *Northern New Spain: A Research Guide*. Tucson: University of Arizona Press, 1981.

Bolton, Herbert Eugene. *The Mission as a Frontier Institution in the Latin-American Colonies*. El Paso: Texas Western Press, 1962.

————. *Padre on Horseback*. Reprint ed., Chicago: Loyola University Press, 1963.

————. *The Rim of Christendom*. New York: Macmillan, 1936.

————. *The Spanish Borderlands*. New Haven: Yale University Press, 1921.

Borhegyi, Stephen F. de, and others. *El Santuario de Chimayó*. Santa Fe: The Spanish Colonial Arts Society, Inc. 1956.

Boyd, E. *Popular Arts of Spanish New Mexico*. Santa Fe: Museum of New Mexico Press, 1974.

Bunting, Bainbridge. *Early Architecture in New Mexico*. Albuquerque: University of New Mexico Press, 1976.

Castañeda, Carlos E. *Our Catholic Heritage in Texas, 1519–1936*. San Antonio: Von Broeckmann - Jones Company, 1936.

Cook, Sherburne Friend. *The Conflict Between the California Indian and White Civilization*. Berkeley: The University of California Press, 1943.

Dana, Richard Henry. *Two Years Before the Mast: A Personal Narrative*. Boston: Houghton Mifflin Company, 1884.

Dickey, Roland F. *New Mexico Village Arts*. Albuquerque: University of New Mexico Press, 1970.

Espinosa, José E. *Saints in the Valley: Christian Sacred Images in the History, Life and Folk Art of Spanish New Mexico*. Revised edition. Albuquerque: University of New Mexico Press, 1967.

Geiger, Maynard J., O.F.M. *The Life and Times of Fray Junípero Serra*. Washington, D.C.: Academy of American Franciscan History, 1955.

Gregg, Josiah. *Commerce of the Prairies*. Norman: University of Oklahoma Press, 1954.

Habig, Marion A. *The Alamo Chain of Missions*. Chicago; Franciscan Herald Press, 1968.

Hewett, Edgar L., and Fisher, Reginald G. *Mission Monuments of New Mexico*. Albuquerque: University of New Mexico Press, 1943.

Hildrup, Jesse S. *The Missions of California and the Old Southwest*. Chicago: A. C. McClurg & Company, 1912.

Horgan, Paul. *Lamy of Santa Fe: His Life and Times*. New York: Farrar, Straus and Giroux, 1975.

Jackson, Helen Hunt. *Father Junípero and the Mission Indians of California*. Boston: Little, Brown & Company, 1902.

————. *Glimpses of Califora and the Missions*. Boston: Little, Brown & Company, 1902.

Jenkins, M. E. and Schroeder, A. H. *Brief History of New Mexico*. Albuquerque: The University of New Mexico Press, 1974.

Jones, Oakah L., Jr. *Los Paisanos: Spanish Settlers on the Northern Frontier of New Spain*. Norman: University of Oklahoma Press, 1979.

Kessell, John L. *The Missions of New Mexico Since 1776*. Albuquerque: The University of New Mexico Press, 1979.

————. *Friars, Soldiers and Reformers: Hispanic Arizona and the Sonoran Mission Frontier, 1767–1858*. Tucson: The University of Arizona Press, 1976.

Morfi, Juan Agustin. *History of Texas, 1673–1779*. Los Angeles: Quivira Society, 1935.

Pérez de Villagra, Gaspar. *History of New Mexico by Gaspar Pérez de Villagra, Alcala, 1610*. Trans. by Gilberto Espinosa. Los Angeles: Quivira Society, 1933.

Picazo, Luis and others, *La Iglesia de Santa Cruz de la Cañada*. Privately published, 1983.

Prince, Lebaron Bradford, *Spanish Mission Churches of New Mexico*. Reprinted. Glorieta, New Mexico: Rio Grande Press, 1977.

Riesenberg, Felix. *The Golden Road, The Story of California's Mission Trail*. New York: McGraw-Hill, 1962.

Ruxton, George F. *Adventures in Mexico and the Rocky Mountains*. Reprint ed., Glorieta, New Mexico: Rio Grande Press, 1973.

Simmons, Marc. *New Mexico: A Bicentennial History*. New York: W. W. Norton & Company, 1977.

Spicer, Edward H. *Cycles of Conquest: The Impact of Spain, Mexico and the United States on the Indians of the Southwest, 1533–1960*. Tucson: University of Arizona Press, 1962.

Tinkle, Lon. *Six Missions of Texas*. Austin: Texian Press, 1965.

Twitchell, Ralph Emerson. *The Spanish Archives of New Mexico*, vols. 1 and 2. New York: Arno, 1976.

Weber, David J., ed. *New Spain's Far Northern Frontier: Essays on Spain in the American West, 1540–1821*. Albuquerque: University of New Mexico Press, 1979.

Weigle, Marta, ed. *Hispanic Arts and Ethnohistory in the Southwest*. Santa Fe: Ancient City Press, 1983.

Yoakum, H. *History of Texas: From its First Settlement in 1685 to Its Annexation by the United States in 1846*. San Antonio: The Steck Company, 1935.

Index